LEGAL PRACTICE MANAGEMENT
AND QUALITY STANDARDS

To Kate and Susan

LEGAL PRACTICE MANAGEMENT AND QUALITY STANDARDS

Craig Evan Klafter, BA (Hons), MA, D Phil (Oxon)

and

Gordon Huntley Walker, BA, FIPD, FIQA, FAQMC, MASQC

BLACKSTONE
PRESS LIMITED

Published in Great Britain 1995 by Blackstone Press Limited,
9-15 Aldine Street, London W12 8AW. Telephone 0181-740 1173

ISBN: 1 85431 323 1

British Library Cataloguing in Publication Data
A CIP catalogue record for this book is available from the British Library

Typeset by Style Photosetting Limited, Mayfield, East Sussex
Printed by Livesey Limited, Shrewsbury, Shropshire

Contents

Acknowledgements

Quality is not something that one arrives at overnight. We owe a great debt to friends, colleagues and clients who have helped us over many years towards a broader understanding of quality.

This book had its beginnings in consultancy work undertaken by us as members of Gordon Walker & Associates, a firm of quality management consultants based in Plymouth. Although the firm has helped companies secure ISO 9000 registration for over a decade, its foray into legal practice management came in 1992 when the Legal Section of the South Hams District Council retained us to help it implement an ISO 9001 quality system. The total professionalism of all those who worked in that section in tackling project problems with commitment and dedication as they arose encouraged us to continue providing quality assurance consultancy to the legal profession. Since that time, we have advised numerous companies, firms and government organisations. We are grateful to all our clients for providing us with the valuable experience that has gone into this book.

Our thanks are also due to the numerous organisations which have given us assistance. The Lord Chancellor's Office gave their ready advice and provided relevant information on legal practice management systems. The Law Society provided useful insight into the historical development of solicitors' interest in quality assurance. The International Organisation for Standardisation (ISO) granted permission to reproduce Chapter 4 of ISO 9001. The Association of Quality Management Consultants (AQMC) was a useful source of information on consultancy practices. The Institute of Quality Assurance (IQA) gave us a forum to present ideas on legal practice management and obtain useful feedback. Those who attended our IQA course entitled 'BS 5750, TQM and the Legal Community' gave us ideas, support and encouragement.

We would like to thank our wives for their constructive suggestions, support and encouragement throughout.

Introduction

This is a book of practical advice, not a theoretical textbook; it is intended to show legal practitioners how to set about adopting professional quality assurance standards without spending a fortune or losing their way.

Adherence to quality assurance standards has become a requirement for the practice of law, and legal practitioners are now being required to develop, document and implement quality assurance systems. When they approach the subject, they see many seemingly different and apparently conflicting standards. In the United Kingdom, the Legal Aid Board has recently required franchisees to implement quality assurance principles and the Law Society has become the first professional association of lawyers in the world to adopt Practice Management Standards based on quality assurance principles. Several local authorities are planning to require ISO 9000 registration as a prerequisite to allowing firms to tender for legal services. Some companies have requested that the firms they retain obtain ISO 9000 registration. These initiatives are all the result of demands by bulk purchasers of legal services, including corporations, public bodies and financial institutions, seeking assurances that the firms they retain are properly managed and thus provide value for money. While lawyers tend to perceive these initiatives as being independent of each other, they are all based on common quality assurance principles.

Quality assurance is good business. As competition within the legal community becomes more and more severe, practitioners need to use every means at their disposal to succeed. Perhaps the easiest way in which a lawyer's practice can be made more competitive is by improving the manner in which the practice is managed. This is particularly important at a time when firms are expanding, merging and establishing satellite offices. In the United States, where this trend reached its peak during the 1980s, only a small percentage of firms have been successful in maintaining the size they once achieved. Whereas mergers and acquisitions by law firms were commonplace then, split-offs and down-sizing are more typical today. Among the firms who have been unsuccessful in maintaining their expanded form, the predominant reason for failure, according to the American Bar Association Legal Practice Management Section, was inadequate legal practice management. As practitioners in other countries consider similar business changes in their search for competitive advantage, they would do well to heed the lessons to be learned from their American counterparts and seek to establish better management systems. The search for improved methods of legal practice management has led forward-thinking lawyers throughout the world to realise the wisdom of relying on quality assurance systems, widely tried, tested and adopted within manufacturing and service industries, to help them improve their practice management.

Requiring adherence to such systems, however, is not an attempt by business and government to impose costly bureaucratic standards on the legal community. The application of quality assurance to the legal profession will improve profitability for those practices which introduce it. Poor quality is expensive. The implementation of quality management systems means that a legal practitioner has more time to devote to chargeable hours, exposure to malpractice liability is lessened and clients are more likely to be satisfied with, and offer repeat business to, the practice. ISO 9000, as an internationally recognised standard, will also help to secure foreign business and make cross-border firm mergers easier to manage and sustain.

This book addresses the predominant question being asked by lawyers today — how does a practice develop, document and implement a quality assurance system to meet ISO 9000 requirements? In answering this question, the book explains the principles which lie behind all of the quality assurance standards, goes on to clarify the application of the principles to legal work, and shows the reader how to develop, draft and implement uncomplicated systems which will meet the requirements of ISO 9000 and help meet other quality assurance standards, giving straightforward examples and advice. It goes on to outline, and guide the reader through, the ISO 9000 registration process.

Chapter 1

Quality Assurance as a Management Tool

A quiet revolution, based on quality assurance, has been taking place in business since the early 1980s. It is aimed at improving organisational performance by concentrating on giving a better product and service to the customer. For many businesses, this represents a radical change from traditional thinking. The traditional approach was to concentrate on the improvement of profits by looking inward and trying to reduce overhead costs — often by using obsolete systems and machinery and by making little investment in new methods, training or equipment. In contrast, the quality assurance approach improves organisational performance by directing the organisation to look outward to find out what its customers actually want and are prepared to pay for. People are usually happy to pay more for good-quality goods and reliable services; not only that, but they will come back with repeat business to places where they can be sure of finding them. It costs less and it is easier, for any business, to have existing customers come back than to go out trying to find new ones.

Quality assurance is led from the top of any organisation and involves all levels of staff in an open-minded approach to exploring problems, looking for root causes rather than instant solutions. It is a change in the way businesses are managed and operated. It is not easily achieved. Staff with the necessary skills and enthusiasm have to be developed and encouraged. The simple motive of the need to survive has been the spur to action for many organisations.

QUALITY ASSURANCE DEFINED

Quality is 'the totality of features and characteristics of a product or service that bear on its ability to satisfy stated or implied needs' (ISO 8402). Traditionally, quality has been associated mainly with manufactured products but in recent years there has been a rapidly increasing emphasis on quality as applied to the supply of services in both the public and private sectors. This is evinced by the Citizen's Charter and public service performance standards in the United Kingdom, and a conscious effort by many private service businesses, internationally, to improve their customer service and thereby their public reputations. Indeed, more service

organisations than manufacturing organisations are currently registered to international quality systems standards. This all leads to a greater general awareness
amongst the public that poor goods and services are no longer things that have to
be tolerated and that quality is easily obtained by selective buying.

Central to the concept of quality is making sure that the purchaser is satisfied
with the goods or services supplied. From a consumer's point of view, quality is
based on a few simple precepts:

(a) Quality means: something that is fit for purpose. For example, a small compact
car, though inexpensive to buy, can be a quality car. Running costs, such as fuel, spares
and maintenance are usually low. It is useful for shorter trips, takes up little space and is
ideal for someone who wants a town car. A limousine is also a quality car (although a
good deal more expensive) for, say, a visiting diplomat. Neither of these, however, is of
much use to a farmer who needs a powerful four-wheel drive vehicle of robust
construction to cope with the demands of ploughed fields and hillsides.

(b) Quality means: something that is on time. For example, in manufacturing
industry today, increasing emphasis is being placed on the 'just in time' principle.
In order to save warehousing costs, and to avoid having to pay for major supplies
before they are needed, a manufacturer does not want goods delivered too early.
On the other hand, late delivery would mean that production schedules would
suffer, cash flow would be affected and customers might be lost. The solution is to
demand that they arrive 'just in time'.

'Just in time' is also essential to service industries. The manager of a group of
consultants will assign tasks to individual consultants based on their specialisa-
tions. Each consultant needs to complete his or her work before the manager can
write a general report for the client. If the specialised consultants complete their
work too early, they risk having their manager rely on out-of-date information or
analysis. If the specialised consultants complete their work too late, the manager
will have insufficient time to complete the report to the client. The 'just in time'
concept applies equally well to service industries as it does to manufacturing.

(c) Quality means: getting things right first time. This is sometimes taken to
imply that everything should be done to perfection straight away. Instead, it means
that people are trained, and any process is adjusted, to ensure that it becomes easy,
and the norm, for everything to be done right. For example, a play is usually well
performed on its opening night, but an audience does not see the effort, difficulties
and corrections that went into the numerous rehearsals. Consistency of output is
also implied; it should be possible to see the play on its thousandth performance
and find it as well performed as on its first.

(d) Quality means: value for money. A customer wants a fair price without
hidden costs. So far as is possible, a customer wants to know the costs of
ownership of an item, or the total costs of a service, at the outset of any transaction.
If value for money is obtained, the customer comes back — that means more
turnover, profit, security and growth for the supplier.

The ability of a business to offer value for money is highly dependent on keeping the hidden costs to a minimum. For example, if a service provider has a high level of failure and waste, then it is the customers who ultimately have to pay for that inefficiency. This, in the end, means no new work and no repeat work for that business.

(e)   Quality means: meeting the agreed, and the implied, specification. If you buy a railway ticket then, broadly speaking, the agreed specification is that the railway will transport you from A to B. The implied specification is that it will also carry you safely, in reasonable comfort and will arrive on time.

(f)   Quality means: reliability. Prospective customers look for the ability of a product or service to continue to function satisfactorily, simply, and in an environmentally-friendly manner at a consistent performance level, with a minimum of stoppages, changes, servicing or maintenance.

(g)   Quality means: customer satisfaction. A supplier should achieve all the above with genuine knowledge and understanding of the customer's needs, without argument, time wasting, warranty claims, complaints or excessive effort on either side.

Before entrusting important business to a concern, customers want to be confident that the quality of the service or product required will be provided reliably, consistently, on time and at the right price. Some of the ways they may seek to establish this confidence would be: to look for evidence that the business is registered to an independently assessed quality standard; to ask others about the quality of service provided, and to look for a documented statement that sets out the organisation's operating policy. The demonstration, prior to the production of an end-product or service, of how a business is organised, how it uses its professional or technical capability and how it meets its promises, is known as quality assurance.

These ideas of judging the quality of goods or services by means of customer satisfaction can readily be applied to legal services. A lawyer may be considered to be 'fit for purpose' if he or she has the professional competence necessary to undertake the matter being assigned. This not only includes appropriate legal qualifications, knowledge and experience; it also includes the practical skills necessary for client relations, administrative management and financial management. A practitioner's 'fitness for purpose' is also determined by the ability to meet the expressed and implied terms of the agreement under which services were retained. Such agreements usually contain an understanding of the time necessary to complete the assigned work. Consequently, a lawyer's ability to provide the necessary service in a timely and efficient manner is essential to achieving client satisfaction. Lastly, a practitioner must provide value for money. This involves quoting a reasonable hourly rate for work undertaken, handling a matter efficiently, providing clients with regular accounting of billed time and expenses, keeping them informed about the progress of a case, being responsive to the client's needs and being accessible for further instructions. All of these factors bear on a practitioner's ability to satisfy the client and provide a quality service.

Who is responsible for quality? The answer is simple — everyone. Consider the way that any business activity is undertaken. There is a chain of people involved where each person is dependent on another. For example, a lawyer's handling of a case is dependent on ability to instruct subordinates and colleagues accurately about the facts of the case and the work that needs to be done. This ability, in turn, often depends on the typing and distribution of clear information and on instructions from the client.

This interdependence is referred to, in quality assurance terms, as the 'internal customer' concept: every employee identifies a customer or customers within an organisation and finds out what those customers want. In terms of the above example, the lawyer is the customer of the secretary who types the information and the secretary is the customer of the messenger who delivers the information. All should accurately determine what their customer wants and should work to satisfy those needs. This sounds easy, but is not; there are often cultural barriers that can prevent easy and informal communications.

'Suppliers' (people who supply goods or services for a consideration), whether internal or external, must avoid making assumptions about their customers' wants — 'leaping to confusions'. The only way to find out what their customers really want is to ask them. This is not always easy — sometimes the answers are not what they want to hear! Quality assurance is dependent on clear and open (even fearless) communication between members of staff at all levels. The significant factor here is that the cost of putting things right once they have gone wrong rises exponentially as any case progresses (figure 1.1). Making sure that things are right at the outset (instruction review, or 'contract review' in quality assurance terms) can save a great deal of time, effort and money later on.

Responsibility for quality assurance systems is reflected by a practice's organisational structure. Senior partners or senior management establish policies (e.g., one policy could be that of a practice conforming to the requirements of ISO 9000) and strategies to pursue those policies (e.g., a policy of only instructing outside counsel in writing and a strategy of placing copies of counsel's instructions in the case file). Fee-earners have an obligation to implement those policies and strategies and to perform work to professional standards. Employees involved in support services must work to standards established by the practice. Most importantly, the secretaries and managing partners of a practice should ensure that all operations are client-focused. This means that every decision regarding a practice's work must be considered from the viewpoint of the client's convenience and benefit. Every function, every person, every change, influences the client's perception of the quality of a practice's work.

Responsibility for quality cannot just be individually oriented; it must also be collective. The principal enemy of quality assurance is the pointing finger, where individuals or organisations all attempt to disclaim responsibility for a failure by

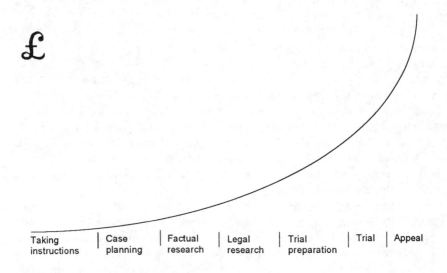

| Taking instructions | Case planning | Factual research | Legal research | Trial preparation | Trial | Appeal |

Figure 1.1   The cost of corrective action

blaming someone else. Quality assurance management requires that failures be brought into the open and investigated by looking for inadequate management systems, incomplete training or unclear instructions rather than for an incompetent individual — looking for root causes and documenting corrective actions. The good sense of this is borne out by many studies of failures in various industries. Most failures, by far, are caused by poor management systems, poor communications and unrecorded changes to existing arrangements, not by individuals.

Similarly, if the enemy of quality is the pointing finger, the friends of quality are enthusiasm and expectations. If management can lead from the front with vision and high expectations, clearly communicated, of where the practice is going and the quality of work the practice should produce from well-paid and well-motivated employees, those employees will almost invariably respond in a positive fashion. They will not only maintain high standards in the work they do but will also attempt to help others meet the high standards required — a synergy of effort. The importance of the individual to an organisation, however, must not be underestimated: it often takes only a minor individual failure (e.g., an improperly filed document or incorrectly cited case) to negate the quality of an entire practice.

In considering the role of the individual, individual creativity and style also bear on quality assurance. Lawyers' styles vary, different clients prefer different styles, and all of this adds to a practice's versatility and reputation. A quality assurance system need not cramp creativity or style; it simply adds to effectiveness by giving efficient support and an organisational framework within which to operate.

In order to understand the current movement towards the concept of quality assurance as a management tool, and its relevance to the practice of law, it is helpful to consider the history of its development. Even before the Industrial Revolution, the concept of quality was concerned with the craftsman's ability to design and create work to the satisfaction of an individual customer. Like all quality work, it required planning and the application of skill. Acceptance standards were initially agreed by discussion between buyer and seller. In order to detect fraud, and to guarantee the work, the ideas of inspection, standard measures and general quality standards were introduced. Some of these standards (e.g., the Egyptian unit of length was standardised prior to 1550 BC), and markings to indicate quality achievements, (e.g., masons' marks on cathedrals) have existed for centuries. British hallmarks have acted as a safeguard to purchasers of gold and silver articles for over six centuries.

After the Industrial Revolution came a much wider need for standardised products, and the services needed to support them, since the direct communication between buyer and seller often no longer existed. In manufacturing industries inspection by an independent function was the accepted solution; service organisations used a hierarchy of supervision to fulfil the same function. Inspection, however, is an inefficient way of checking work. It may set one person against another because they often have a different understanding of requirements. It operates after the work is done and only sorts good work from bad, rather than preventing mistakes. It costs money but does not add value. Moreover, inspection tends to become less accurate as the volume of work increases.

It was war which led to the development of quality assurance techniques. The war effort for World War I required manufacturers to produce vast amounts of munitions in record time. All these munitions had to be interchangeable; for example, every bullet had to fit any gun for which it was made, anywhere in the world, under any conditions. The old methods of guaranteeing quality were not suited to the situation. Due to the personnel demands of the war effort, there were insufficient numbers of available inspectors. Moreover, many of the products required repeatability of performance, not just dimensional accuracy (e.g., every unit of ammunition must fire reliably and must be of a shape necessary to ensure firing accuracy). Quality assurance was the concept developed to respond to this situation.

Quality assurance management is based on the theory that if you cannot test the quality of every item produced then you test the system that produces the items. In that way you can assure the quality of the items the system produces. Quality assurance management guarantees the quality of a good or service through the use of common sense and systems (see figure 1.2). Such systems were first developed in the United States as 'Military Standards' (MIL-STDs) in the first half of the 20th century. While these specifications dominated the American defence industry, few people in non-defence work, either there or in other countries, saw the advantages in using them.

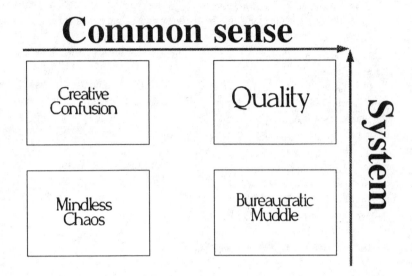

Figure 1.2

Then, at the end of World War II, when the Japanese were endeavouring to restore their steel and coal industries, two leading American quality assurance gurus, W. Edwards Deming and Joseph M. Juran, visited Japan to help rebuild their manufacturing base. Up until that time, Japanese industry had been associated only with cheap, inferior goods. These men started a quality assurance movement which the Japanese credit with transforming their economy. In the 50 years since the war, Japanese manufacturers have used quality assurance management techniques to capture world markets from other countries including shipbuilding and motorcycle manufacturing from the United Kingdom, cameras from Germany and televisions and radios from the United States. As an indication of the debt Japanese manufacturers owe to quality assurance management, the most coveted management award in Japan today is the Deming Prize.

Since 1960, quality assurance management has become increasingly internationalised. In the 1960s, the United Kingdom applied MIL-STDs to some of its defence work, and NATO later used them to develop Allied Quality Assurance Publications (AQAPs). The United Kingdom Ministry of Defence followed by improving on the NATO standards, developing its own 'Defence Standards' (DEF STANs). The weakness of all of these was that they applied only to defence work, and the British Standards Institution sought to apply similar standards to all industries by publishing BS 4891 (Guides to Quality Assurance) and the first issue of BS 5750, a quality system specification capable of general application. In July 1982, the British Department of Trade published the white paper called *Quality,*

Standards, and International Competitiveness which concluded that a great deal of work to improve quality was required within all sectors of British industry to make it internationally competitive. As a result of much effort, and in the face of many conflicting interests, BS 5750 (henceforth to be known internationally as ISO 9000) was finally agreed upon by about 60 countries as the common international quality assurance standard in 1987.

ISO 9000 is the first international quality assurance standard. It establishes quality requirements for 20 key categories of a business operation, and embodies the basic elements of a quality assurance system. The text of the standard is identical in every country apart from the language used and each country's own identifier. While originally designed for application to manufacturing concerns, it has increasingly been applied to service-oriented organisations including doctors, engineers, accountants, advertising agencies, government and lawyers. Compliance with the standard is assessed by independent, government-approved certification bodies which authorise businesses to use their quality logo.

QUALITY ASSURANCE STANDARDS

The international standard ISO 9000 is the most elementary quality assurance standard that a lawyer can use to guide the installation of a quality assurance system. It prescribes that a practice's quality assurance system covers 20 distinct areas of business operations. It is relatively easy to comply with, is internationally agreed upon, has an established registration process and is widely recognised.

Total quality management (known as TQM, or TQ) is a more comprehensive quality assurance initiative. Total quality management may be defined as a style of management that generates a culture aimed at ensuring that everyone gets everything right first time every time. It is based on three components: client-focused improvements (both internal and external); a documented quality system (usually provided by ISO 9000); and management and staff commitment, involvement and attitude change toward continuous improvement.

Although total quality management is more comprehensive than ISO 9000 and is a worthy future quality assurance goal, it is not suited to a practice's first foray into quality assurance management. There is no single internationally adopted standard and TQM can therefore mean many different things to different people. It is not as widely recognised and there is no registration process. ISO 9000 is the preferred introduction to quality assurance management and will serve as a solid foundation for practices seeking to comply with a more stringent standard.

The cornerstone of compliance with any quality assurance standard is having a documented quality assurance system, comprised of three elements (see figure 1.3). A quality assurance manual expresses the quality policy or objectives the practice wishes to attain, contains positive statements regarding the standards to which the practice operates, and outlines the capability of the practice and that of its practitioners. This manual serves several purposes. It can be used as an in-house

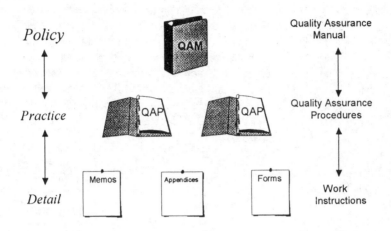

Figure 1.3   A documented quality system

standard document for reference, for the training of new employees, and as a marketing tool to send to major clients with a view to informing them of the practice's versatility, experience and quality of operation.

The quality assurance procedures (of which there may be several, depending on the size and complexity of the practice) explain the management systems put into practice to meet those policies or objectives. Ideally, each should explain why the procedure is necessary, what activities it covers, who is responsible for what and the rules governing how a particular task is to be carried out. Work instructions, where necessary, supplement in detail how those procedures should be implemented. In its entirety, the documented quality assurance system describes how a practice is managed.

A quality assurance system is important to a legal practice because it facilitates giving the client confidence, based on a positive and responsible declaration about the quality and reliability to be expected from the practice. It is an important and powerful marketing tool, since reputation for quality of service is central to a lawyer's ability to attract and maintain clients.

Quality assurance registration in accordance with ISO 9000 will help a practitioner secure work because prospective clients are seeking the demonstrable assurances that accompany objective third-party assessment to a defined international standard. Quality assurance is central to reducing professional liability exposure since most claims arise from simple and obvious errors that could have been avoided if quality systems were in operation. Having to develop policies and procedures in order to introduce quality assurance to a practice can also provide a focus for better organisational leadership, practitioner teamwork and employee job satisfaction.

There are also some less obvious benefits: some practices have found that speaking the language of ISO 9000 gives confidence to those clients who already have it and allows the practice to get on with the job without continual checking up and wasting time. More precise instructions are usually forthcoming from such clients, and information may be put to better use. More precise instructions can also be given to subcontractors, such as counsel, which in turn can lead to the development of a more efficient working relationship. Client complaints can be dealt with more effectively; it is often not the complaint but the fact that it is not dealt with that causes the real dissatisfaction.

The most important benefit which quality assurance can give a practice is that of helping it to achieve greater efficiency and economy by reducing failure and appraisal costs (see figure 1.4).

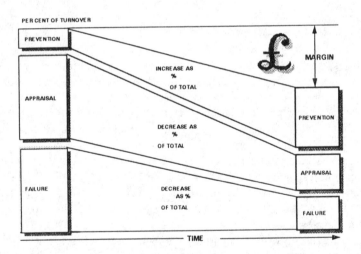

Figure 1.4   Cost of quality as a percentage of turnover

Failure costs are incurred when things go wrong and work is either scrapped altogether or has to be redone. These costs can be subdivided into external and internal costs. External failure costs are where the client is dissatisfied and the lawyer has to spend time satisfying and answering client complaints, or where loss of reputation or goodwill is involved. Internal failure costs are caused by inefficiently leaping from crisis to crisis because of ineffective systems, trying to control events, and reinventing policies because no one ever bothered to write them down. All failure costs are also the costs of lost opportunities, since while damage-limiting activities are going on, the most important activity, that of developing the business, is being neglected.

Appraisal costs may be considered as being the costs of inspection, where a practitioner has to take time to double-check the work of subordinates and conduct management reviews and audits, and maintenance costs, such as keeping a reference library. However, a relatively minor investment in prevention can significantly reduce these failure and appraisal costs. Prevention includes determining policies for the conduct of the business, writing and implementing procedures which translate those policies into practice, planning ahead to meet business requirements and training people from the start in how the business operates — quality assurance. Prevention is an investment and, as with any other investment, it must show a dividend. The dividend it shows is that it drives down the costs of appraisal and failure. The resultant margin is achieved without engaging any extra people, without any marketing, without any extraordinary effort — by working smarter, not harder.

Chapter 2

The Legal Community's Interest in Quality Assurance

An organisation's interest in quality assurance management can usually be traced to a combination of two reasons. The first is that the market demands it; the second is that people within an organisation realise that quality assurance management can help them to address important management issues (e.g., productivity, efficiency, cost control). The legal community is no exception in this regard.

Beginning in the late 1980s, market forces required the legal community to review the quality of its service. The Legal Aid Board, the largest bulk purchaser of legal services within the United Kingdom, was faced with rocketing costs during the late 1980s and early 1990s. Between 1990 and 1993, for example, there was a 35.4 per cent annual increase in Legal Aid Board expenditure on legal services. In response to this, the Board demanded that solicitors who undertake legal aid work improve the efficiency of their service.

The Legal Aid Board decided to experiment with requiring practitioners to implement quality assurance management systems. The Board initially set up a franchise experiment in Birmingham using six firms of solicitors. The idea of the franchise system was to delegate decision-making powers to grant legal aid, in exchange for certain quality guarantees by the franchisee. The quality guarantees cover a number of areas including: general facilities, experience of supervisors, case administration, file management systems, training requirements, and work submitted to the area office. In the opinion of the Legal Aid Board, the franchise experiment was a success.

In October 1992, the Legal Aid Board continued its initiative by publishing *Franchising: the Next Steps* which set out the Board's policy objectives with regard to franchising and the application of quality assurance to legal aid work. The essential elements of the scheme, as explained by the Board, were: the reduction of the administrative costs of suppliers of legal services and an improvement in the service offered to their clients, the specification of quality assurance standards; the arrangement of audits by the Board to ensure that the standards are achieved; the control of case costs; the establishment of review procedures where contracts were refused or revoked, and the creation of a continuous monitoring system to ensure the scheme achieved its objectives. The Legal Aid Board also announced that 'where an applicant has achieved BS 5750 [now ISO 9000] certain of the requirements in this document may not be audited'. Once policy objectives were defined, the Board needed to establish a means of appraising practitioners against these objectives.

In December 1992, the Legal Aid Board published *Transaction Criteria* which is essentially a checklist against which the professional competence of a practice is compared. For example, with regard to case files, it prescribes that files should include, in part, the client's name, the client's address and a unique identifying number. The reason for this basic approach is that the criteria are designed to be used by quality auditors who, for the most part, lack prior legal experience. *Transaction Criteria* embodies a system of grading the quality of a solicitor's practice according to one of the following standards: excellence, competence-plus, threshold competence, inadequate professional services or non-performance. The December 1992 *Transaction Criteria* covers only green form/ABWOR and emergency civil legal aid work. Criteria for other areas of legal aid work will be published in the near future.

The final stage in the Legal Aid Board's efforts to impose quality assurance management on the legal community began in April 1993 when the Board published *Franchising Specification: Draft for Consultation* offered as a 'partnership with the profession to provide an accessible and quality assured legal aid service'. This draft was quickly followed in July 1993 by the fully approved version, *Franchising Specification*, which sets out the arrangements for the introduction of franchising. The essential elements of the scheme are: an improvement in the service offered by suppliers of legal services to their clients and the reduction of their administrative costs; the specification of quality assurance standards; arrangements for audits; control of case costs; an effective appeal procedure; continuous monitoring of the scheme, and obtaining the views of clients about franchised organisations. The application process began on 1 October 1993.

At present, the Legal Aid Board's quality initiative is primarily directed at solicitors, but there are strong suggestions that, in time, it will be extended to others within the legal profession who undertake legal aid work. Indeed, even without an attempt by the Board to extend this initiative to others within the legal community, solicitors who participate in the franchise scheme will need to seek quality assurances from those they instruct, including barristers, expert witnesses, conveyancers etc. The Legal Aid Board is doing its best to practise what it preaches. It has commenced its own internal quality drive and the Leeds Legal Aid Board, for example, has secured ISO 9000 registration.

As the largest bulk purchaser of legal services within the United Kingdom, the Legal Aid Board constitutes the principal market force affecting the legal community. Others, such as local authorities and companies, are also looking at quality assurance. Local authorities are considering requiring ISO 9000 registration as a prerequisite to tendering for local authority work. Likewise, companies which have achieved ISO 9000 registration are asking retained outside counsel to meet the standard as well. Given the increasingly competitive market for legal services, ISO 9000 is becoming an essential tool for the success of many legal practices.

In addition to these market forces, internal reasons for improving the quality of the solicitor's profession were becoming apparent. The most obvious concerned the number of client complaints filed against solicitors. In 1990, for example, there were 20,000 client complaints filed with the Solicitors Complaints Bureau. These complaints covered four principal areas including (a) delay, (b) lack of information, (c) negligence and (d) dishonesty. While there were, no doubt, multiple complaints filed against individual solicitors, the fact that the profession was only 60,000 strong indicates the gravity of the problem.

To the Law Society's credit, it quickly responded to this situation by adopting r. 15 of the Solicitors' Practice Rules on client care, which was introduced in 1990 to be effective in 1991. This practice rule effectively constituted the first quality assurance standard universally imposed on the English and Welsh legal community. It requires: the operation of a complaints handling procedure; that clients are informed of who is handling their case, and that clients are informed of issues raised and the progress of the case. The Law Society adopted this rule in the hope that it would lessen the number of complaints being filed against members of the profession.

While the practice rule on client care was a positive start, it incorrectly supposed that the problem was only one of perception and poor communication. The reality was that the level of client complaints was symptomatic of deeper practice management problems. At the core of this was the belief among most solicitors that no problem existed and thus nothing needed to be done. One of the first signs of this attitude became apparent between July and September 1992 when the Solicitors Complaints Bureau conducted a survey of 800 firms regarding their implementation of r. 15 and concluded that the rule was being flouted. Veronica Lowe, Solicitors Complaints Bureau Director, responded by issuing a statement in the *Gazette* which reminded solicitors that sanctions exist for breaching the rule and warned that tougher enforcement was on the horizon.

Rule 15 was not the only attempt by the Law Society to improve the quality of its membership. In February 1991, the Law Society in conjunction with the British Standards Institute published *Quality: a Briefing for Solicitors and BS 5750 Code of Quality Management for Solicitors*. This document, which came into being as a result of pressure from the Legal Aid Board and some Law Society members, was an attempt to interpret BS 5750 (now ISO 9000) for application to the practice of law and was aimed at improving the standard of quality of all solicitors' practices. However, it did not mandate that solicitors comply with the standard. Indeed, the Law Society indicated some scepticism about the application of a manufacturing standard to the legal profession.

As a whole, *Quality: a Briefing for Solicitors and BS 5750 Code of Quality Management for Solicitors* is an excellent introduction to BS 5750 (now ISO 9000) and its application to the practice of law. The document, however, has some limitations. The reader gets the distinct impression that the British Standards Institute is the only registration body. This is simply not true. There are numerous accredited registration bodies who are experienced in registering legal service organisations. The reader is also given the impression that the interpretation of BS 5750 (now ISO 9000) presented in the document is the only interpretation which exists. The fact is that the interpretation rendered in the document is the British Standards Institute's interpretation. Other registration bodies may have their own interpretation or may be more willing to accept an interpretation presented by the organisation seeking registration. While the Law Society document on BS 5750 (now ISO 9000) is an excellent guide, it should not be viewed as being definitive.

Two additional developments showed the legal community at large that quality assurance management could help them address important management issues. One prominent firm of solicitors implemented ISO 9000 and another total quality management respectively. In 1991, Pannone March Pearson of Manchester became the first firm of solicitors in England to earn ISO 9000 registration. The immediate benefits that the firm noted were a reduction in client inquiries, more precise work instruction, a reduction in malpractice liability, better control over and better relations with counsel, an improved working environment and public relations benefits. In the words of Andrew Simpkin, corporate divisional partner, 'the great benefit of BS 5750 [now ISO 9000] is that you can demonstrate to the outside world that you have been looked at objectively by a third party, and can provide a quality service'. Within a few months of registration, Mr Simpkin realised that clients were 'not follow[ing] the time-honoured British approach of continually checking up and consequently wasting our time'.

While Pannone Marsh Pearson pioneered ISO 9000 registration by solicitors, Buss Murton sought in 1992 to achieve the tougher requirements of Total Quality Management. The immediate benefits they noted included: continuous and significant improvement in workload and new clients; a 25 per cent reduction in telephone bills and calls received; considerable improvement in staff morale and efficiency; and a significant reduction in the number of complaints received. Robert Sedgwick, managing partner of Buss Murton, summarised the success of Total Quality Management, thus: 'It works because it is simple and it helps us to achieve our goals by providing a structure and a discipline. Above all it means we can provide clients with a true quality service'. The success of both these firms in meeting their respective quality assurance goals served as a beacon to the profession. Their accomplishments brought the application of quality assurance management to legal practice from the realm of theory to the real world. Most importantly, solicitors now had proof of the real benefits quality assurance management could bring.

These developments heralded the legal community's growing interest in quality assurance management, but a crisis occurring at the beginning of 1993 sparked the Law Society into taking bolder action. In January 1993, the Law Society reported that the Solicitors Indemnity Fund, the fund which insures solicitors' clients against wrongdoing by their solicitor, was in serious trouble. The report indicated that there had been a record number of claims totalling £58.6 million during 1992 and, as a result, all solicitors were required to make extra contributions to shore up the fund. The most noteworthy conclusion of the report, from the point of quality assurance, was that only 10 per cent of all claims arose from lack of knowledge of the law and a smaller percentage arose from fraud. The greatest number of claims were caused by simple and obvious errors which might have been avoided by better organisation or office management.

This situation forced the Law Society to realise that stronger action had to be taken on the quality assurance front. In February 1993, the Law Society published a consultation paper titled *Practice Management Standards* which was designed to serve as a practical management tool for the benefit of solicitors and their clients. It provided guidelines against which practices could measure the way they managed themselves, and a checklist for planning improvements and developments. It established quality assurance standards covering the following areas of a practice's operation: case management, office administration, financial management, managing people, the firm's services, forward planning and management structure. These standards were consistent with Legal Aid Board requirements and are closely linked with ISO 9000 and total quality management.

In April 1993, the Law Society's Council approved practice management standards which were published in June 1993 under the title *Practice Management Standards: Managing for Success*. This document not only included the quality assurance standards introduced in the consultation paper but also included a guide to implementation. In publishing these standards, the Law Society expressed the hope that 'improving quality of office and case management, by following the standards, should lead to profitability and success'. The two reasons behind this assumption were: (a) the 'organised and professional approach to management and administration advocated by the standards will reduce the risk of mistakes and wasted effort' and (b) 'in an increasingly competitive climate, the standards will help practices provide services that meet clients' requirements and expectations, encouraging repeat business'. Thus, the Law Society became the first professional body of lawyers in the world to adopt quality assurance standards.

The external benefits of compliance with these standards were soon realised. The Legal Aid Board announced in July 1993 that it had adopted all relevant parts of the Law Society's *Practice Management Standards* into its franchising specifications and Sun Alliance Insurance Group and several Lloyd's of London insurance syndicates reported that they would provide premium discounts of up to 20 per cent on professional indemnity insurance for firms who met recognised quality assurance standards. Future developments are likely to bring additional benefits since bulk purchasers of legal services including local authorities, major companies and even the European Community are considering requiring ISO 9000 before allowing firms to tender for business. A practice's ability to meet recognised quality assurance standards has become essential for any firm seeking to succeed in this time of increased competition for legal services work. The benefits of quality assurance management will not only be realised in terms of a firm's ability to provide efficient legal services but will become a valuable marketing tool.

Chapter 3

The ISO 9000 Standards

The ISO 9000 standards form an internationally adopted quality assurance specification series. As of 1994, nearly all industrialised countries have agreed to the specifications including all of Europe, North America and most of the Far East. The standards are identical in all countries apart from local language translation and a country specific identification code in those countries which wish to use one. (For example, ISO 9000 is identified as BS EN ISO 9000 in the UK.) As international standards, they are ideal for firms seeking to expand practice into other countries, for ISO 9000 registration is a useful international marketing tool

The ISO 9000 series contains management system requirements that must be established and documented by an organisation such that an independent assessor can be assured that the organisation's quality system is effective. The specifications do not dictate to what level an organisation must operate nor do they require an organisation to adopt specific management systems. Rather, the specifications require an organisation to establish and document its own quality standards and then document and implement 20 areas of management systems which, if adhered to, will result in the organisation meeting those standards. This means that it is possible for an individual practice to set its own quality objectives and operate its own unique management systems.

The ISO 9000 series was originally written for manufacturing organisations, since it was in manufacturing that quality assurance principles had their beginnings. It contains five distinct but complementary standards: ISO 9000, ISO 9001, ISO 9002, ISO 9003 and ISO 9004. The first and last of these give guidance on the use of the other three, where ISO 9001 is intended for a design and development operation; ISO 9002 for a production and installation operation; and ISO 9003 for an inspection operation. This, however, does not mean that the standards are not of value to service organisations such as a legal practice. There are sufficient similarities between all types of businesses to make the application of these standards to service organisations worthwhile; indeed the series itself contains guidance for applying the standards to service organisations, in ISO 9004. Nevertheless, it requires careful interpretation for application to the practice of law before a practice can seek to comply with it. Since the practice of law requires original planning suited to each client's needs, ISO 9001 : 1994 is the most appropriate model for lawyers and is the one which will be explained herein.

The first step in interpreting ISO 9001 : 1994 for application to the practice of law is to understand its terminology. The terms may be interpreted as follows:

Customer: client (or 'internal customer').
Supplier: legal professional (or 'internal suppliers').
Product: professional services provided to the client.
Contract: the recorded and agreed understanding of legal services required by a client, including the action to be taken, the terms of business and the nature of any follow-up.
Delivery: completion or disposal of a matter.
Design control: planning the progress of a case.
Subcontractor: supplier of goods and/or services to the practice.

The following is a section-by-section interpretation of ISO 9001 : 1994's application to the practice of law beginning with the first procedural standard which appears as chapter 4. Chapters 1 to 3 provide definitional and reference information which has already been described above. Chapter 4 of the standard is reproduced in its entirety in Appendix I.

ISO 9001 : 1994 INTERPRETED FOR APPLICATION TO THE PRACTICE OF LAW

4 QUALITY SYSTEM REQUIREMENTS

4.1 Management responsibility

4.1.1 Quality policy
The partnership of a practice must formally define and document a quality policy and standards which it aims to achieve. The partnership must ensure that this policy and these standards are understood, implemented and maintained by all members of the practice. This requirement may be fulfilled by producing a quality assurance manual (see 4.2.1) which includes a general statement of quality policy and specific statements with regard to each paragraph of ISO 9001. Everyone in the organisation must understand and comply with the contents of the quality assurance manual.

4.1.2 Organisation

4.1.2.1 Responsibility and authority The responsibility, authority and the inter-relation of all members of the practice and employees who undertake work which affects the practice's work product must be defined and documented. The recommended means of fulfilling this requirement is to include in the quality assurance manual an organisation chart listing all fee-earners and support staff. The chart should include a brief job description for each person and the chain of supervisory responsibility.

4.1.2.2 Resources The partnership must make sure that sufficient resources and people are assigned to ensure that the quality assurance system can be maintained, monitored and audited. This requirement does not have to be burdensome. Most practices will find it sufficient to assign responsibility for quality assurance to one person in addition to his or her normal duties, and to establish a modest budget to cover associated costs. These costs will easily be recouped through cost savings initiated as quality assurance is implemented.

4.1.2.3 Management representative The practice must appoint a partnership representative who will have responsibility for the quality assurance system. It is recommended that a partner be appointed quality assurance director.

4.1.3 Management review
The partnership must undertake documented reviews to ensure that:

(a)   the quality assurance system complies with ISO 9001;
(b)   any weaknesses in the practice's management are eliminated;
(c)   quality activities comply with the arrangements specified in the quality assurance manual and quality assurance procedures; and
(d)   that the quality assurance system continues to be suitable and effective for the practice.

It is recommended that these reviews are based on the results of the internal quality audits described in 4.17.

4.2   Quality system

4.2.1 General
A practice must establish and maintain, in a systematic way, a documented quality system which can be easily followed and implemented. It is recommended that the documented quality system comprises a quality assurance manual (which establishes policy, standards and responsibility), quality assurance procedures (which describe the systems in place to achieve the standards) and, where appropriate, detailed instructions (which detail how to use the systems).

4.2.2 Quality system procedures
The practice shall prepare and implement a documented quality assurance system consistent with the requirements of ISO 9001 and the practice's stated quality policy.

4.2.3   Quality planning

The practice shall define and document how the requirements for quality stated in the policy will be met. The practice shall give consideration to the following activities in fulfilling client instructions:

(a)   the preparation of quality plans;
(b)   the identification and acquisition of appropriately trained personnel and necessary publications, equipment and resources;
(c)   the suitability of quality systems to the work undertaken;
(d)   the modification of quality systems as necessary;
(e)   the identification and acquisition of required expertise and materials not available within the practice in sufficient time to fulfil client needs;
(f)   the verification of materials at appropriate stages;
(g)   the clarification of legal requirements; and
(h)   the identification and preparation of quality records.

4.3   Instruction review

4.3.1   General

A practice must establish and maintain procedures for taking instructions from clients which ensure that:

(a)   client instructions are clearly defined and confirmed in writing;
(b)   changes are agreed in writing with the client; and
(c)   the practice is capable of fulfilling the client's instructions (in that it has the expertise, manpower and has no conflicts of interest).

4.3.2   Review

All client instructions must be reviewed to ensure that:

(a)   the requirements are adequately defined and documented;
(b)   there is a meeting of the minds; and
(c)   the practice has the capability to fulfil the client's needs.

4.3.3   Amendment to a contract

Changes in instructions must be confirmed with the client.

4.3.4   Records

Records of instruction reviews must be maintained.

4.4   Design control

4.4.1   General

A practice must establish and maintain procedures to control cases undertaken by the practice in order to ensure that client instructions are met.

4.4.2   Design and development planning
The practitioner responsible for a particular case must draft, and update when necessary, a quality plan which:

    (a)   outlines the work to be performed;
    (b)   identifies the goods and services required to complete the case;
    (c)   specifies who has responsibility for aspects of the case; and
    (d)   indicates important dates or deadlines.

Cases must be allocated to people who are capable, qualified and provided with adequate resources to undertake the work involved.

4.4.3   Organisational and technical interfaces
If more than one practitioner is undertaking work on a case, the need to share information must be identified and the necessary information must be documented, transmitted and regularly reviewed.

4.4.4   Design input
Legal requirements relating to the progress of a case must be identified, documented and their relevance reviewed by the practitioner for accuracy. Ambiguous or conflicting legal requirements must be resolved or brought to the attention of the client.

4.4.5   Design output
Work product must be documented and expressed with reference to the quality plan, relevant legal requirements and the instructions of the client so that the progress of a case can be measured at any time by a person not involved in the case. It is recommended that a time recording system which includes brief descriptions of work undertaken in terms of the quality plan is maintained. It is also recommended that a system for recording and describing expenses pertaining to a case is maintained.

4.4.6   Design review
There must be documented reviews of the progress of a case at appropriate stages. Participants at such reviews must include all fee-earners working on the case and, if appropriate, the client.

4.4.7   Design verification
Quality plans should be verified by a practitioner not responsible for the case who is competent with respect to the area of law covered by the case. Verification must establish that the quality plan meets all relevant legal requirements and conforms to client instructions.

4.4.8   Design validation
All forms and court submissions must be checked to make sure that they conform with legal requirements.

4.4.9   Design changes
A practice must establish and maintain procedures for the identification, documentation and verification of all changes and modifications to the quality plan. The client must be informed of any alterations.

4.5   Document and data control

4.5.1   General
A practice must establish and maintain procedures to control all documents and data that relate to the documented quality system.

4.5.2   Document and data approval and issue
Prior to issue, documents and data must be reviewed and approved for adequacy by the partnership representative for quality assurance, or by personnel working under the supervision of and with the authority of the partnership representative. Relevant quality assurance documents must be made available at all locations where operations essential to the functioning of the quality system are performed (e.g., practitioners are given copies of all quality assurance documents which concern their work performance). Obsolete documents must be promptly removed from all points of issue or use (or assured against unintended use, e.g., by marking them 'obsolete — for record purposes only'). Note that it is permissible to have identified uncontrolled copies of quality assurance documents for marketing purposes. Uncontrolled copies do not have to be updated and maintained in accordance with quality assurance system requirements.

4.5.3   Document and data changes
Changes to quality assurance documents must be reviewed and approved by the partnership representative responsible for quality assurance, or by personnel working under the supervision of and with the authority of the partnership representative. All personnel involved in the review and approval process must have access to pertinent background information upon which to base their decisions. Where practicable, an explanation of all changes or modifications must be identified in the relevant quality documents. A master list must be established to record and identify the revision of all quality assurance documents in order to preclude the use of superseded documents or procedures. Documents must be reissued after a significant number of changes have been made.

4.6 Purchasing

4.6.1 General
A practice must ensure that purchased goods and services conform to specified requirements.

4.6.2 Evaluation of subcontractors
A practice must select suppliers of goods and services (e.g., outside counsel, expert witnesses, office supplies providers) on the basis of their ability to meet specified requirements, including quality requirements, established by the practice. A practice must establish and maintain records of acceptable suppliers (see 4.16). The selection of suppliers, and the type and extent of quality system controls exercised by the practice, shall be dependent upon the type of goods or services and, where appropriate, on quality audit reports and/or quality records of suppliers' previously demonstrated capability and performance. A practice must ensure that the suppliers' quality system controls are effective.

4.6.3 Purchasing data
Purchasing documents must describe the goods or services ordered, including, where applicable as determined by the practice:

   (a)   a detailed and precise identification of the product ordered (e.g., 92295A Hewlett Packard LaserJet toner cartridge — black);
   (b)   a detailed description and explanation of requirements of services ordered (e.g., written instructions to outside counsel specifying the work to be undertaken, who is to be performing it, legal requirements and relevant deadlines); and
   (c)   the relevant requirements of ISO 9000 to which a supplier must conform so as to ensure the quality of the goods or services supplied.

A practice must review and approve purchasing documents for adequacy of specified legal requirements and case needs prior to release.

4.6.4 Verification of purchased product

4.6.4.1 Supplier verification at subcontractor's premises
Where a practitioner chooses to verify the work of subcontractors (e.g., expert witnesses, barristers, conveyancers, consulting engineers) at the subcontractor's place of business, the practitioner must specify verification arrangements and the terms of work in written instructions.

4.6.4.2 Customer verification of subcontracted product
Where specified in the purchase contract, a client or a representative of the client must be afforded the right to verify at source or on receipt that goods or services purchased on the

client's behalf conform to the specified requirements. Verification by a client does not absolve the practice of its responsibility to provide to the client acceptable goods or services nor shall it preclude subsequent rejection. When the client or a representative elects to carry out verification, such verification must not be used by the practice to absolve it of its responsibility to maintain effective quality control over the supplier of goods or services.

4.7 Control of customer-supplied product

A practice must establish and maintain procedures for verification and, where relevant, storage and maintenance of goods and services purchased on the client's behalf and held for the client's benefit. Any goods or services that are lost, damaged or are otherwise unsuitable for use must be recorded and reported to the client (see 4.16).

4.8 Product identification and traceability

A practice must establish and maintain a case reference system which, at all times, allows any employee to be able to identify and trace all information, correspondence and material relating to a case. All files must have a unique recorded identification number (see 4.16).

4.9 Process control

A practice must maintain a case-monitoring system to ensure that work on a case is planned, maintained and performed under controlled conditions. Controlled conditions must include:

(a) documented, detailed instructions defining the manner in which work is to be conducted, where the absence of such instructions would adversely affect quality (these instructions may specify the use of suitable equipment, working environment, quality plans and compliance with client instructions or legal requirements);

(b) monitoring, control and approval of cases in progress; and

(c) criteria for assessing the quality of work produced which must be stipulated, to the greatest practicable extent, in written standards or by means of representative samples.

Where a lawyer produces work product which will be used by the client after the client is invoiced for the lawyer's services (e.g., the lawyer drafts a standard lease which the client intends to use for future letting, estate planning), continuous monitoring and/or compliance with documented procedures is required to ensure that initial client instructions and legal requirements are met.

4.10   Inspection and testing

4.10.1   General

Legal practitioners must verify all information and services they use in providing legal services as conforming to specified requirements detailed in the quality plan, client instructions, the law or documented procedures.

4.10.2   Receiving inspection and testing

Where information or services are used in providing legal services prior to being properly verified (e.g., as a result of an emergency or urgent need), legal practitioners must positively identify and record the information or service (see 4.16) in order to permit immediate recall or replacement in the event of non-conformance to specified requirements. The most obvious application of this requirement to the practice of law is where a client is the source of unsubstantiated information which, in time, may turn out to be inaccurate.

4.10.3   In-process inspection and testing

During work on a case, a legal practitioner must verify that his or her work and the work of anyone reporting to him or her conforms to the requirements of client instructions, the quality plan, the law and documented procedures. A legal practitioner must not release work product until the required verification has been completed. A legal practitioner undertaking work on a case must identify any work product which does not conform to specified requirements.

4.10.4   Final inspection and testing

The legal practitioner responsible for a case must undertake a final review of it to ensure that all verification previously specified has been carried out and that the results meet the requirements of client instructions, the quality plan, the law and documented procedures. Cases must not be closed until all the activities specified in the quality plan or documented procedures have been satisfactorily completed and the associated data and documentation are available and authorised.

4.10.5   Inspection and test records

A practice must establish and maintain records which show that all legal work undertaken has been verified as meeting the criteria established by client instructions, relevant quality plans, legal requirements, documented procedures and the quality assurance manual. Since the legal practitioner responsible for a case is responsible for ensuring that inspection and test requirements are met, the recommended means of complying with this standard is for senior partners of a practice to assess each practitioner periodically to make sure that they comply with these requirements. These assessments should be complemented by regular spot checks of each practitioner's work product.

4.11   Control of inspection, measuring and test equipment

4.11.1   General
A practice must maintain, or have easy access to, a legal reference system sufficient to allow practitioners to engage in their practice competently.

4.11.2   Control procedures
All legal reference materials used by the practice, including on-line services, statutes, reports, loaned material and in-house generated materials (e.g., memoranda and briefs), must be catalogued, kept up to date and properly stored. A practice must maintain or have easy access to such reference equipment and software (e.g., Lexis, microfilm readers, computer databases) as is required to practise law completely and must have personnel properly trained on such equipment and software. Where reference equipment or reference software is used, they must be checked at prescribed intervals to prove that they are serviceable. A practice must establish the extent and frequency of such checks and must maintain records as evidence of control which must be made available to clients on request.

4.12   Inspection and test status

The inspection and test status of work product must be identified, throughout a case, using markings which will ensure that only work product that has passed the required inspections and tests is dispatched or used. Markings must identify who carried out the inspection and authorised the work product's release or use. The recommended method for meeting this requirement is to have the person undertaking inspection initial or sign the product after it is approved.

4.13   Control of nonconforming product

4.13.1   General
A practice must establish and maintain procedures to ensure that if work product is non-conforming (e.g., an early draft of a contract), it is marked as such (e.g., 'superseded document') and not used.

4.13.2   Review and disposition of nonconforming product
A practice must establish who has responsibility for controlling non-conforming product. This will usually be the person undertaking inspection (e.g., the practitioner assigned to do the work). Where non-conforming work product is unintentional, it must be brought to the attention of the person or persons who produced the work to determine the reason(s) for the non-conformance.

4.14   Corrective and preventive action

4.14.1   General
A practice must establish and maintain documented procedures for implementing corrective action.

4.14.2   Corrective action
The procedures for corrective action must include:

(a)   the effective handling of client complaints and reports of inadequate work product;

(b)   investigation and documentation of the cause of complaint or inadequate work product;

(c)   determination of the corrective action needed to eliminate the cause of nonconformities; and

(d)   verification that corrective action is taken and is effective.

4.14.3   Preventive action
A practice must establish, document and maintain procedures for investigating the cause/s of non-conforming work product and the action needed to prevent recurrence. These should include the analysis of all processes, systems and client complaints to detect and eliminate potential causes of non-conforming work product, and initiation of preventive actions to deal with problems to a level corresponding to the risks encountered.

4.15   Handling, storage, packaging, preservation and delivery

4.15.1   General
A practice must establish, document and maintain procedures for handling, storage, packaging and delivery of all documents, data and materials used in, held by and generated by the practice.

4.15.2   Handling
A practice must provide methods and means of handling that prevent damage or deterioration to documents and material.

4.15.3   Storage
A practice must provide secure storage areas or stockrooms to prevent damage or deterioration of documents or materials, pending use or delivery. A practice must properly deposit in a financial institution any funds supplied to it on a client's behalf. Appropriate methods for authorising receipt and the dispatch to and from such areas or such financial institutions must be stipulated (e.g., recording who has withdrawn a file from a file room and when that person either returns it or transfers

it to another). (This ISO 9000 accounting requirement is considerably less strict than that required by most professional legal associations (e.g. the Law Society's Solicitors' Accounts Rules).) In order to detect deterioration, the condition of stock supplies must be assessed at appropriate intervals (e.g., inventory of document files).

4.15.4 Packaging
A practice must control binding, packing and marking of documents, materials and funds to the extent necessary to ensure conformance to specified requirements from the time of receipt until the practice's responsibility ceases.

4.15.5 Preservation
All documents, materials and funds must be identified, preserved and segregated whilst under the practice's control.

4.15.6 Delivery
A practice must arrange for the protection of the quality of documents, materials and funds after final inspection and test. Where contractually specified, this protection shall be extended to include delivery to destination.

4.16 Control of quality records

Quality records must be identified, collected, indexed (where appropriate, with reference to the case involved), filed, safely stored and maintained to demonstrate the effectiveness of the quality assurance system. Pertinent subcontractor quality records must be an element of these data. Retention times of quality records must be established and recorded. Where agreed contractually, relevant quality records must be made available for evaluation by the client or a representative of the client for an agreed period.

4.17 Internal quality audits

A practice must carry out a comprehensive system of planned and documented internal quality audits to verify whether quality activities comply with planned arrangements and to determine the effectiveness of the quality system. The partnership representative responsible for quality must periodically review the system. Quality auditors must not audit the activity they are responsible for. Quality audits should take place at least annually. The audits and follow-up actions must be carried out in accordance with documented procedures. The results of the audits must be documented and brought to the attention of the personnel having responsibility in the area audited. The management personnel responsible for the area shall take timely corrective action on any deficiencies found by the audit. Follow-up audits must check the effectiveness of that corrective action, and the results of audits form an integral part of the management review process.

4.18   Training

A practice must establish and maintain procedures for assessing training needs and provide for the training of all personnel performing activities affecting quality. Personnel performing specific assigned tasks must be qualified on the basis of appropriate education, training and/or experience, as required. Appropriate records of training (including continuing legal education requirements) must be maintained.

4.19   Servicing

Where after-care is specified in original instructions (e.g., as a result of a retainer) or merited because of the nature of the legal work undertaken (e.g., estate planning), a practice must establish and maintain procedures for performing follow-up work and verifying that it is carried out in accordance with specified requirements.

4.20   Statistical techniques

4.20.1   Identification of need
If it is not practical to carry out adequate quality checks of every item of output then it will be necessary to check random samples using statistical techniques (e.g., reviewing the chargeable hours of fee-earners in comparison to the work produced (quality in terms of value for money), Pareto analysis, statistical process control, etc.).

4.20.2   Procedures
A practice must establish documented procedures for implementing and controlling adequate statistical techniques required for verifying the quality of legal service provided.

Chapter 4

How to Draft a Quality Assurance Manual in Compliance with ISO 9001 : 1994

The first step towards the introduction and development of a documented quality assurance system is to ensure that the partners of the practice are of one mind about its introduction. Management commitment is the mainspring of successful introduction and operation of any business strategy. If senior people are not convinced of the advantages of a documented quality assurance system, then those advocating the introduction should not move until they are; otherwise the quality assurance system will fall apart at some later stage and credibility will be lost. Analysis of many failed business improvement schemes has demonstrated that the lack of senior management commitment is one of the most frequent causes of failure.

Drafting a documented quality assurance system in compliance with ISO 9001 : 1994 requires examination of current operating practices against each of the standard's requirements. A practice will see where current policies are already consistent with the standard, where new policies have to be determined and where modifications are needed. A practice's stated quality assurance system policy, which appears in a quality assurance manual ('QAM'), constitutes the first part of the documented quality assurance system.

The main function of the QAM is to define the quality system structure, that is, to show how, by reference to policies, procedures, organisation and responsibilities, the practice intends to meet the requirements of ISO 9001 : 1994. It may also, however, be used to demonstrate the capabilities of the business. This last is sometimes neglected, but can be extremely important to the practice: the QAM can be used as a powerful sales or marketing tool, setting out as it does what the quality policies are, how the business is organised, and what the capabilities of the firm are. Copies may be sent to major clients or to prospective clients as part of a marketing programme. Some practices choose not to distribute copies of the QAM fearing that it will divulge too much information to competitors. In doing so, they deprive themselves of significant benefits. Provided the potential marketing use is considered in drafting the QAM, there need not be any exposure of confidential information.

Other advantages of having a QAM include those of having a central reference to the practice's quality system for the training of new employees, and for reference to the practice's policies and approach to quality. Setting out the QAM and endorsing it as a formal statement of policy ensures that proper understanding and acceptance of the principles involved are recognised and accepted at the highest level. Most importantly, it means that things have been thought through.

While a model quality assurance manual follows, it is not recommended that a practice merely change the names and adopt it as their own. A quality assurance manual should be as unique as the practice. It describes the structure and manner in which a firm operates. Trying to operate your practice using another practice's quality assurance manual is like trying to rule Britain with the United States Constitution; Britain would not be the same. The best approach to developing a quality assurance manual is to follow the instructions contained herein and draft your own.

The front page should set out the name and address of the practice whose QAM it is and may be as stylish as desired for maximum effect — remember, it may be used as a marketing tool. It may include some reference to confidentiality on the front. A suitable form of words would be: 'This manual and the information contained therein is the property of [name of practice]. It must not be reproduced in whole or in part or otherwise disclosed without prior consent in writing from [name of practice].'

The format of the manual is optional, although A4 page size in loose-leaf form in ring-binders can be recommended. It is to be expected that there will be many changes to the contents in the early days of the manual, so a format which lends itself to easy changing is required. A page numbering, issuing and amendment system should be devised, and described in the QAM, such that it is clear at any time whether all the pages are there and that they are current. The distribution of the manual, and who is responsible for its control, maintenance and allocation, should be described, and a distribution list should be kept separately as part of a master document control system.

There should be a contents list covering the entire document. A comprehensive manual should include, for example:

(a)   an introduction which sets out how the QAM is organised,

(b)   a policy statement,

(c)   nomination of a management representative,

(d)   the scope of the practice's activities under, for example, the headings of: the activities, the facilities available to the business and the staffing profile,

(e)   the organisation, responsibility and authority and interrelationship of those with executive responsibility for quality,

(f)   sections dealing in general terms with each requirement of the ISO standard in turn, stating whether or not it applies to the business and, if so, how it will be applied,

(g) cross-references between the QAM, the procedures and the ISO standard,
(h) a list of the associated quality assurance procedures for the practice,
(i) a glossary of ISO terms and their QAM definitions as applied to the practice,
(j) any reference documents.

A policy statement for insertion in the manual should make reference to the applicable standard, and a typical statement might read as follows:

It is the established policy of [name of the practice] to operate a quality assurance system that will fully meet the requirements of ISO 9001 : 1994 and to supply professional services which fully satisfy the agreed client requirements. Management is committed to the achievement and maintenance of high standards of professional practice and client care within a wide range of legal activities, and to the provision of premier services, competitive on price, quality and delivery, to their clients. They recognise, and act upon, the principle that achieving this depends upon the wholehearted cooperation, motivation and involvement of the practice's entire team so as to promote the confidence, trust and dependability which are the hallmarks of the relationship between professional staff and client. The importance of the quality system to the success of the practice is recognised by the appointment of [name of significantly senior or competent person] as the practice's management representative. This manual, together with its supporting documentation, defines the practice's requirements for quality and the means to satisfy these requirements. The objective of the documented quality system is to ensure that work, whilst not forsaking individual style, is carried out in a planned, effective and consistent manner; fostering, and not inhibiting, the exercise of professional judgment and creative problem solving. The quality assurance system shall be continually and systematically reviewed for effectiveness and improvement. No deviation from these directions is permitted without the authority of the management representative.

Signed .... (by the managing partner)

The next section of the QAM, describing the scope of the practice's activities, should give details of the background of the practice and what work can be undertaken, together with any particular expertise which may be available to clients. The facilities available could be described, including the situation of the offices and the equipment available such as computers, the reference library, and any other items which might demonstrate an efficient and client-responsive approach to the business of a law practice. Similarly, the numbers of staff and a précis of their expertise should prove helpful.

In describing the organisation, it is best to include an organisation diagram showing reporting structures and areas of activity, even though this may change from time to time. The principal responsibilities, authority and interrelationships of the practice should be described as part of the body of the text.

The remainder of the quality assurance manual is a statement of a firm's policy commitment to each of the ISO 9001 : 1994 requirements. A quality assurance manual which covers the following material would comply with these requirements:

SECTION 1   Introduction
SECTION 2   Quality Assurance Policy Statement
SECTION 3   Scope of the Practice's Activities and Facilities
SECTION 4   Organisation and Quality Assurance Responsibilities
SECTION 5   Quality System
SECTION 6   Instruction Review
SECTION 7   Project Control
SECTION 8   Quality Document Control
SECTION 9   Purchasing
SECTION 10   Client-supplied material
SECTION 11   Identification and Traceability
SECTION 12   Work Monitoring
SECTION 13   Verification of Work
SECTION 14   Legal Reference System
SECTION 15   Verification Monitoring
SECTION 16   Problem Reporting
SECTION 17   Remedial Action
SECTION 18   Safeguarding of Documents and Materials
SECTION 19   Quality Records
SECTION 20   Internal Quality Audits
SECTION 21   Training
SECTION 22   Work Follow-up
SECTION 23   Statistical Techniques
SECTION 24   Cross-references to ISO 9001 : 1994 and the Documented Quality Assurance System
SECTION 25   List of Quality Assurance Procedures
SECTION 26   Glossary
SECTION 27   Reference Documents

What follows is a sample Quality Assurance Manual which incorporates all of the above suggestions.

HITCHCOCK, SIMPSON, HARGRAVE, COKE & LITTLETON
HITCHCOCK HOUSE
46 HIGH STREET
LONDON SW1 4GH

Telephone 0171-555 1212
Facsimile 0171-555 1213

QUALITY ASSURANCE MANUAL

This manual and the information contained herein is the property of Hitchcock, Simpson, Hargrave, Coke & Littleton. It must not be reproduced in whole or in part or otherwise disclosed without prior consent in writing from Hitchcock, Simpson, Hargrave, Coke & Littleton.

ISSUE: A
COPY NO: 1 of 10
Copyright © 1994 by Hitchcock, Simpson, Hargrave, Coke & Littleton
Prepared by S.P. Littleton, August 1994

HITCHCOCK, SIMPSON, HARGRAVE, COKE & LITTLETON
QUALITY ASSURANCE MANUAL

AMENDMENT PROCEDURE

All amendments to this Manual must be authorised by the Management Representative.

Manual and procedural changes shall not be implemented until amendments are
formally issued.

Each amendment shall be introduced by the issue of a new page or pages for
each controlled copy in existence.

The issue number of each amended page shall be incremented and dated.

Details of all changes shall be recorded on the amendment record, which will
be reissued with each change.

DISTRIBUTION OF THE MANUAL

Quality assurance manuals are classified as controlled and uncontrolled. Controlled
copies are identified on the title page by the copy number. Uncontrolled copies are
not numbered, are printed on green paper, but are otherwise identical to controlled
copies at the time of issue.

Controlled copies are issued to all those named in Section 4.1 on the authority
of Mr R.T. Hitchcock, who is responsible for both issue and revision.

Uncontrolled copies may be distributed on the authority of Mr. S.P. Littleton;
distribution is unrestricted and these copies will not be revised or amended.

HITCHCOCK, SIMPSON, HARGRAVE, COKE & LITTLETON
QUALITY ASSURANCE MANUAL

AMENDMENT RECORD

Note: Mr S.P. Littleton is responsible for maintaining this record.

Amendment number	Section number	Page number	Issue number	Date	Authorisation

HITCHCOCK, SIMPSON, HARGRAVE, COKE & LITTLETON
QUALITY ASSURANCE MANUAL

CONTENTS

HITCHCOCK, SIMPSON, HARGRAVE, COKE & LITTLETON
QUALITY ASSURANCE MANUAL

SECTION 1

INTRODUCTION

This manual describes the organisation of Hitchcock, Simpson, Hargrave, Coke & Littleton and defines the procedures for the maintenance of the firm's quality assurance system.

The quality assurance system is organised to comply with the requirements of ISO 9001 : 1994, *Quality Systems — Model for Design, Development, Production, Installation and Servicing*.

This manual is supported by quality assurance procedures which are listed in section 25.

Procedures and work instructions are written to give specific details of methods of compliance with requirements expressed in the manual.

HITCHCOCK, SIMPSON, HARGRAVE, COKE & LITTLETON
QUALITY ASSURANCE MANUAL

SECTION 2

QUALITY ASSURANCE POLICY STATEMENT

It is the established policy of Hitchcock, Simpson, Hargrave, Coke & Littleton to operate a quality assurance system that will fully meet the requirements of ISO 9001 : 1994 and to supply professional services which fully satisfy the agreed client requirements.

The Partner's are committed to the achievement and maintenance of a high degree of professional competence and client care within a wide range of legal activities, and to the provision of premier services, competitive on price, quality and delivery, to their clients. They recognise, and act upon, the principle that achieving this depends upon the wholehearted cooperation, motivation and involvement of the Firm's entire team so as to promote the confidence, trust and dependability which are the hallmarks of the professional relationship between solicitor or conveyancer and client.

The importance of the quality system to the success of the practice is recognised by the appointment of Mr R.T. Hitchcock as the Firm's management representative.

This manual, together with its supporting documentation, defines the Firm's requirements for quality and the means to satisfy these requirements. The objective of the documented quality system is to ensure that work, whilst not forsaking individual style, is carried out in a planned, effective and consistent manner; fostering, and not inhibiting, the exercise of professional judgment and creative problem solving.

The quality assurance system shall be continually and systematically reviewed for effectiveness and improvement.

No deviation from these directions is permitted without the authority of the management representative.

HITCHCOCK, SIMPSON, HARGRAVE, COKE & LITTLETON
QUALITY ASSURANCE MANUAL

SECTION 3

SCOPE OF THE FIRM'S ACTIVITIES AND FACILITIES

3.1   ACTIVITIES

Hitchcock, Simpson, Hargrave, Coke & Littleton is a legal practice specialising in employment law on behalf of employers. Its subspecialties include:

Employment contracts
European Community law
Collective bargaining
Employee benefits
Discrimination law
Worker's compensation law
Wrongful discharge law
Labour arbitration

The Firm is involved in, and processes, the work and litigation relating to all the above specialised fields.

The Firm has a considerable fund of experience in employment law, and the constituent members have the qualifications necessary to carry out work in all the above areas. Where additional legal or technical advice or assistance is required, such as that provided by outside counsel, appropriate selection criteria are used and the results kept under review to ensure the integrity of the Firm's quality system.

The emphasis of the Firm's business, and the volume, have changed in recent years; from comparatively regular and straightforward operations, to a significant increase in work relating to discrimination and the European Community, together with increasing amounts of litigation, and involvement in a wider range of activities.

Particular attention is paid to work experience and training within the Firm in order to develop individuals and to maximise resources.

The Firm prides itself on having a substantial history of expertise and achievement, yet being flexible to current trends within the legal profession and capable of quick response to customers' needs, giving individual attention and a high standard of capable and courteous service to the client. These factors are fundamental to the Firm's operation.

3.2   FACILITIES

The Firm operates from modern and well-equipped offices in central London. The Firm has an excellent and well-maintained reference library with an updating service, listed reference books, periodicals and law reports, and a current information distribution system. Files and documents are centrally handled from a strongroom and maintained whilst in use by individuals using secure storage in offices. Other resources include a computer network with word processing, spreadsheet, time management, electronic mail and accounting software linking all fee-earners and support staff. Royal Mail and courier services are used for the transmission of external documents, and facsimile facilities are also available.

3.3   STAFF

Hitchcock, Simpson, Hargrave, Coke & Littleton has a staff of nine qualified legal practitioners, two legal assistants, seven support staff and one office manager. The practitioners have a full range of experience ranging through all the activities listed in 3.1.

HITCHCOCK, SIMPSON, HARGRAVE, COKE & LITTLETON
QUALITY ASSURANCE MANUAL

SECTION 4

ORGANISATION AND QUALITY ASSURANCE RESPONSIBILITIES

4.1 MANAGEMENT ORGANISATION

Hitchcock, Simpson, Hargrave, Coke & Littleton Organisational Chart

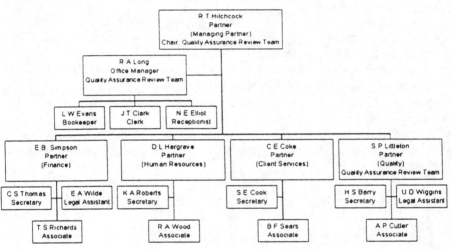

Notes:

(a)   The above diagram is organisational/functional and has no other significance.

(b)   In the absence of a functional representative, senior management shall
assign responsibility elsewhere.

4.2 MANAGEMENT REPRESENTATIVE

The Management Representative with authority and responsibility for ensuring that
the requirements of ISO 9001 : 1994 are implemented and maintained within
Hitchcock, Simpson, Hargrave, Coke & Littleton shall be Mr R.T. Hitchcock.

4.3 QUALITY ASSURANCE RESPONSIBILITIES

4.3.1

Mr R.T. Hitchcock has:

(a) ultimate responsibility for the Firm's policy and objectives for, and commitment to, quality, ensuring that the quality policy is understood, implemented and maintained within the Firm;

(b) overall management responsibility for all functions affecting quality of service to clients, and for the supply of services to client requirements;

(c) responsibility for ensuring that adequate resources exist to meet the quality requirements of the business;

(d) ultimate responsibility for contractual negotiation and client liaison;

(e) responsibility for the organisation of appropriate financial and administrative control procedures;

(f) responsibility for purchasing and subcontractor assessment, ensuring that orders are placed only with approved suppliers, that all orders contain quality requirements, and that purchasing is competitive on pricing;

(g) responsibility for the assessment of work for acceptability, for the assessment of training needs, and for the provision of appropriate training within the Firm.

In addition, he, Mr S.P. Littleton and Mrs R.A. Long together with any members of staff required for particular topics, form the Firm's quality assurance review team.

4.3.2   Fee-earners have individual responsibility for:

(a) the taking of new instructions (instruction review), ensuring that client requirements are clearly understood, that actions to be taken are clear, that the nature of the work and any follow-up are clearly understood by both parties, that the Firm is qualified to perform the work required and that capacity exists to carry out the work within the required time-scale;

(b) the planning, scheduling, review, progressing and reporting, through to completion, of individual cases in accordance with the requirements agreed with the client, using the procedures of the documented quality system and providing a first line of communication and liaison between clients and the Firm;

(c) the selection and use of appropriate subcontract assistance where required (taking advice from within the Firm if necessary), providing instructions and reviewing the work;

(d) the initiation, maintenance and retention of all required quality records;

(e) ensuring that projects are completed within allocated budget costs and within agreed time limits.

4.3.3

Mr S.P. Littleton, in addition to his other duties, has overall responsibility for:

(a)   maintainance of the documented quality system and preparation, allocation and revision of all quality assurance documentation, raising amendments, new procedures, or work instructions as necessary;

(b)   preparation of the Firm's audit and review plan and ensuring that all necessary audits, audit reports and corrective actions are completed;

(c)   allocation of work within the Firm, in discussion with Mr Hitchcock as necessary.

HITCHCOCK, SIMPSON, HARGRAVE, COKE & LITTLETON
QUALITY ASSURANCE MANUAL

SECTION 5

QUALITY SYSTEM

This manual sets out the directions for achievement of the required quality standards.

It is supported by procedures and instructions, and all staff shall ensure that they understand, and are familiar with, the procedures and instructions which are applicable to their work.

In meeting the requirements of any client instructions, consideration shall be given to the need for the production of quality plans and to the client's wishes regarding approval of them and any other documentation.

HITCHCOCK, SIMPSON, HARGRAVE, COKE & LITTLETON
QUALITY ASSURANCE MANUAL

SECTION 6

INSTRUCTION REVIEW

Procedures are maintained for the review of all instructions received by the Firm to ensure that client requirements are adequately defined and documented, that any discrepancies against previous instructions are detected and resolved with clients, and that the Firm has the capacity to meet the contractual requirements.

If a tender for work has been made by the Firm, it shall be ensured that the basis of instructions is consistent with the original tender, or that any differences are resolved with the client.

HITCHCOCK, SIMPSON, HARGRAVE, COKE & LITTLETON
QUALITY ASSURANCE MANUAL

SECTION 7

PROJECT CONTROL

Procedures are maintained to control and verify all aspects of the work process to ensure that specified requirements are met.

Where applicable, each activity will be planned and documented, and the plans will be updated as the activity evolves.

Planning and verification activities are all assigned to qualified personnel, and every effort is made to ensure that they are equipped with resources in keeping with their needs.

Client requirements are identified, documented and reviewed in accordance with established procedures, and any inadequacies or discrepancies are resolved with the client.

A desired result is agreed between client and solicitor, and is documented, reviewed and progressed to ensure that the client's requirements are pursued so far as may be possible in the light of changing circumstances.

Verification of work progress is carried out by qualified and competent personnel in accordance with established procedures.

All quality plan changes and modifications are subject to review and agreement between client and solicitor, prior to implementation wherever possible, and the reasons for changes are identified and recorded.

HITCHCOCK, SIMPSON, HARGRAVE, COKE & LITTLETON
QUALITY ASSURANCE MANUAL

SECTION 8

QUALITY DOCUMENT CONTROL

All documents relating to the achievement of quality are reviewed, approved and controlled in accordance with established procedures. These procedures ensure that pertinent issues of all documents are available where they are needed and that obsolete issues are promptly removed.

A document is 'needed' where its absence is likely to affect achievement of the required standard of quality.

All quality-related documents are numbered and listed in accordance with the document control procedures, and the lists will include the latest issue numbers or letters.

Changes in quality-related documents are reviewed and approved by their original issuing authority. The approving authority will be in possession of all necessary information on which to base the review and approval.

Records are maintained of the circulation and distribution of all quality-related documents, both in-house and externally.

HITCHCOCK, SIMPSON, HARGRAVE, COKE & LITTLETON
QUALITY ASSURANCE MANUAL

SECTION 9

PURCHASING

Procedures are maintained to ensure that purchased items conform to specified requirements, and that subcontracted services (including those of technical experts and barristers) comply with the Firm's quality standards.

Subcontractors are assessed, approved, and selected in accordance with established procedures, and records are maintained for each.

Purchasing documents comply with procedures defining the need for full and clear description of the requirements, are reviewed and approved by competent personnel before dispatch, and records are maintained.

Where applicable to a particular matter, visits to and consultation with the subcontractor may be agreed with the client.

HITCHCOCK, SIMPSON, HARGRAVE, COKE & LITTLETON
QUALITY ASSURANCE MANUAL

SECTION 10

CLIENT-SUPPLIED MATERIAL

All material, documents, funds or data supplied by the client for incorporation into the services provided by the Firm shall be subject to verification and storage procedures. Procedures are established to ensure that such material is catalogued and protected against loss, damage or deterioration when it has been accepted into the care of the Firm.

Where materials and documents are intended to serve as evidence, the client shall be informed if they are not acceptable as such.

If any contract should include services to be provided by the client, the services will be subject to agreed control procedures to maintain the quality standard of the finished contract.

HITCHCOCK, SIMPSON, HARGRAVE, COKE & LITTLETON
QUALITY ASSURANCE MANUAL

SECTION 11

IDENTIFICATION AND TRACEABILITY

Procedures have been established to identify and trace all information and correspondence relating to a matter, including a reference system which ensures that each individual matter has a unique reference number.

HITCHCOCK, SIMPSON, HARGRAVE, COKE & LITTLETON
QUALITY ASSURANCE MANUAL

SECTION 12

WORK MONITORING

All work is carried out under controlled conditions in accordance with established procedures which ensure that the client is kept informed on the progress of matters where appropriate, and that continuity of work is maintained by appropriately qualified staff even in the absence of the nominally responsible person.

Detailed work instructions are provided in all cases where their absence would affect work quality, and processes are monitored by competent personnel in accordance with quality control procedures.

Guidance is available when required, and staff are required to report problems which could interrupt the progress of a matter or adversely affect the quality of service to the client.

HITCHCOCK, SIMPSON, HARGRAVE, COKE & LITTLETON
QUALITY ASSURANCE MANUAL

SECTION 13

VERIFICATION OF WORK

In-house and subcontract work and services are subject to such inspection as is necessary to establish conformance with specified requirements. This monitoring is done in accordance with established procedures, and takes the form of appraisal, checking and review and any other form of quality observation and surveillance necessary to achieve the desired results.

Procedures for quality monitoring are in operation through all stages of work, and are shown, where appropriate, on quality plans. These procedures and plans include instructions to hold the work until any required checks and approvals have been completed by the authorised person.

Final checking procedures include a review of records to ensure that all work that was initially agreed upon has been completed.

All files for completed matters shall be adequately stored and documented for such period as may be required for the subject-matter or as agreed with the client or by law.

HITCHCOCK, SIMPSON, HARGRAVE, COKE & LITTLETON
QUALITY ASSURANCE MANUAL

SECTION 14

LEGAL REFERENCE SYSTEM

A well-stocked Firm library, with an updating service, exists for the review, maintenance, storage, and safe-keeping of relevant legal reference material including reference books, periodicals, journals, statutes, and law reports. Fee-earners are kept informed in the areas of law in which they work, and in the practice and procedures which they use, and a system operates for the distribution of topical information relevant to the Firm's activities. The Firm also has access to materials not held in the library through Lexis and outside law libraries.

HITCHCOCK, SIMPSON, HARGRAVE, COKE & LITTLETON
QUALITY ASSURANCE MANUAL

SECTION 15

VERIFICATION MONITORING

Procedures are maintained to show when files and documents have been checked
and to show that the correct actions have been taken at the right time.

HITCHCOCK, SIMPSON, HARGRAVE, COKE & LITTLETON
QUALITY ASSURANCE MANUAL

SECTION 16

PROBLEM REPORTING

Any faults or problems arising in the course of work are identified, reported to senior staff as appropriate, and recorded in accordance with established procedures for the control of non-conformance.

These procedures provide for immediate remedial action to correct non-conformances and for recording the action taken.

HITCHCOCK, SIMPSON, HARGRAVE, COKE & LITTLETON
QUALITY ASSURANCE MANUAL

SECTION 17

REMEDIAL ACTION

Procedures are maintained to ensure that all problems or non-conformities, whether originating in-house or from the products and services of subcontractors, are reviewed on a regular basis, and action is taken to prevent recurrence.

These procedures are designed to investigate fundamental causes of problems and initiate corrective action, to forecast potential problems and prevent them, and to measure the effectiveness of any action taken.

Where necessary, changes in procedures will be implemented and recorded as part of the corrective action process.

HITCHCOCK, SIMPSON, HARGRAVE, COKE & LITTLETON
QUALITY ASSURANCE MANUAL

SECTION 18

SAFEGUARDING OF DOCUMENTS AND MATERIALS

Procedures are maintained to control handling, confidentiality, security, ready retrieval and storage of all documents and materials, and include consideration of the requirements of any instruction or contract with regard to accessibility, time of retention, format, etc.

Handling, storage, packing and delivery methods are designed to prevent loss, damage or deterioration.

Storage is provided to contain all documents and materials in a manner appropriate to their value, type, condition, application and ability to withstand environmental conditions.

Methods of authorising receipt to and removal from storage areas are specified.

HITCHCOCK, SIMPSON, HARGRAVE, COKE & LITTLETON
QUALITY ASSURANCE MANUAL

SECTION 19

QUALITY RECORDS

Records of all verification findings of the quality system (sections 2, 7, 13 and 20) and the Firm's activities are made and retained as objective evidence of achievement of the required quality standards. Applicable subcontractor records are included.

All quality records are identifiable to work done under the relevant instruction or contract, and are retained in a readily accessible form.

HITCHCOCK, SIMPSON, HARGRAVE, COKE & LITTLETON
QUALITY ASSURANCE MANUAL

SECTION 20

INTERNAL QUALITY AUDITS

Quality audits are scheduled and carried out on a regular basis to verify that quality activities comply with the planned arrangements and to confirm the continued effectiveness of the quality system.

The audits and follow-up actions are controlled by established procedures, and the results are documented and brought to the attention of those responsible for the area audited in each case.

Deficiencies found in these audits are documented and corrective actions are planned, taken, checked and recorded.

The effectiveness of corrective actions is the subject of review procedures and further audits.

HITCHCOCK, SIMPSON, HARGRAVE, COKE & LITTLETON
QUALITY ASSURANCE MANUAL

SECTION 21

TRAINING

Training needs are identified and training is provided for all staff, in accordance with established procedures and Law Society and other professional requirements, to ensure the required level of client service quality. All staff are trained to a level of competence appropriate to their work.

Records of training are maintained in the Firm's personnel records.

HITCHCOCK, SIMPSON, HARGRAVE, COKE & LITTLETON
QUALITY ASSURANCE MANUAL

SECTION 22

WORK FOLLOW-UP

Procedures exist to ensure that, where after-care is part of the original instructions, and/or where a retainer is paid, the agreed follow-up work is carried out and monitored within the quality system.

HITCHCOCK, SIMPSON, HARGRAVE, COKE & LITTLETON
QUALITY ASSURANCE MANUAL

SECTION 23

STATISTICAL TECHNIQUES

Hitchcock, Simpson, Hargrave, Coke & Littleton use appropriate statistical techniques to monitor the quality of service provided.

HITCHCOCK, SIMPSON, HARGRAVE, COKE & LITTLETON
QUALITY ASSURANCE MANUAL

SECTION 24

CROSS REFERENCES TO ISO 9001 : 1994 AND THE FIRM'S DOCUMENTED
QUALITY SYSTEM

| Para. No. | ISO 9001 REQUIREMENTS | The Firm's Documented Quality System | |
		QA Manual	QA Procedure, if required
4.1.1	Quality policy	Section 2	
4.1.2	Organisation	Section 4	
4.1.3	Management review	Section 2	QAP 1
4.2	Quality system	Section 5	
4.3	Contract review	Section 6	QAP 2
4.4	Design control	Section 7	QAP 3
4.5	Document control	Section 8	QAP 4
4.6	Purchasing	Section 9	QAP 5
4.7	Purchaser supplied product	Section 10	QAP 6
4.8	Product identification and traceability	Section 11	QAP 7
4.9	Process control	Section 12	QAP 8
4.10	Inspection and testing	Section 13	QAP 9
4.11	Inspection, measuring and test equipment	Section 14	QAP 10
4.12	Inspection and test status	Section 15	QAP 9
4.13	Control of nonconforming product	Section 16	QAP 11
4.14	Corrective action	Section 17	QAP 12
4.15	Handling, storage, packing and delivery	Section 18	QAP 13
4.16	Quality records	Section 19	QAP 14
4.17	Internal quality audits	Section 20	QAP 1
4.18	Training	Section 21	QAP 15
4.19	Servicing	Section 22	QAP 16
4.20	Statistical techniques	Section 23	

HITCHCOCK, SIMPSON, HARGRAVE, COKE & LITTLETON
QUALITY ASSURANCE MANUAL

SECTION 25

LIST OF QUALITY ASSURANCE PROCEDURES

These procedures represent the second tier of the documented quality system, and define the methods by which the standards manifested in the quality assurance manual are achieved.

These procedures are controlled and issued by the same authority as the quality assurance manual.

QAP 1   Quality System Audit and Review
QAP 2   Instruction Review
QAP 3   Project Control
QAP 4   Quality Document Control
QAP 5   Purchasing
QAP 6   Client-supplied Material
QAP 7   Identification and Traceability
QAP 8   Work Monitoring
QAP 9   Verification of Work
QAP 10   Legal Reference System
QAP 11   Problem Reporting
QAP 12   Remedial Action
QAP 13   Safeguarding of Documents
QAP 14   Quality Records
QAP 15   Training
QAP 16   Work Follow-up

HITCHCOCK, SIMPSON, HARGRAVE, COKE & LITTLETON
QUALITY ASSURANCE MANUAL

SECTION 26

GLOSSARY OF ISO 9000 : 1994 TERMS AND THE QUALITY ASSURANCE
MANUAL DEFINITIONS

Instruction [contract] review: the process of taking instructions from clients, ensuring that both parties are in agreement on requirements, that these are achievable and that they are documented.

Delivery: completion or disposal of a matter.

Inspection and testing: the verification of work.

Management representative: the appointed individual within the Firm who has defined authority and responsibility for ensuring that the requirements of ISO 9001 : 1994 are implemented and maintained.

Non-conformance (also non-compliance): any failure of a product or service to achieve the agreed quality requirements.

Process control (work control): the work-monitoring system/s.

Product: Professional services or physical product (documents — reports, plans, letters, etc.) prepared for, and supplied to, the client by the Firm.

Purchaser: the client — the person/s, employer, authority or organisation from whom the Firm has taken instructions.

Purchaser-supplied product: client-supplied data, material, funds, information or services provided for the use of the fee-earner in the execution of the agreed services.

Purchasing: the purchase of products or services from sub-contractors (q.v.).

Quality: 'the totality of features and characteristics of a product or service that bear on its ability to satisfy stated or implied needs' (ISO 8402). The concept of quality is appropriately expressed as 'fitness for purpose', which here is taken to include considerations of cost-effectiveness and timeliness.

Quality assurance: 'all those planned and systematic actions necessary to provide adequate confidence that a product or service will satisfy given requirements for quality'. (ISO 8402.)

Quality plan: a plan for the conduct of specific items of professional work handled by the Firm, setting out the quality controls, resources and activities relevant to that project or work item.

Quality system: 'the organisation structure, responsibilities, procedures, processes and resources for implementing quality management'. (ISO 8402.)

Subcontractor: any business or individual from whom the Firm purchases or obtains materials or skills, ranging from suppliers of items such as computers or of such skills as training and consultancy, including barristers and technical experts whose advice and opinions are used in providing the Firm's legal services.

Supplier: Hitchcock, Simpson, Hargrave, Coke & Littleton.

HITCHCOCK, SIMPSON, HARGRAVE, COKE & LITTLETON
QUALITY ASSURANCE MANUAL

SECTION 27

REFERENCE DOCUMENTS

ISO 9001:1994, *Quality Systems — Model for Quality Assurance in Design, Development, Production, Installation and Servicing.*
Quality: a Briefing for Solicitors (London: The Law Society, 1991).
Practice Management Standards (London: The Law Society, 1993).

Chapter 5

How to Draft Quality Assurance Procedures in Compliance with ISO 9001 : 1994

The second component of a documented quality assurance system is quality assurance procedures ('QAPs'). Whereas the quality assurance manual is a policy statement of a practice's intention to conform to specific quality assurance standards, QAPs indicate how the systems which have been put into place will ensure that a practice will meet those standards. As an analogy, if a QAM is viewed as a political party platform in that it describes the policy objectives of a party which, if elected, it will enact in the form of legislation, QAPs can be viewed as statutes which explain the methods by which the government aims to conform to its platform obligations. Some statutes are sufficient on their own; others require regulations to carry them into effect. Likewise, some QAPs require detailed work instructions to ensure that employees comply.

Work instructions are best suited to routine and repetitive work and are not required by ISO 9001:1994. They can, however, be useful to practices which have a high turnover of support staff. In this situation, work instructions can be a useful training tool. Work instructions can be most effective when reduced to a flow chart. For example, figure 5.1 is a flow chart which describes the task of making a cup of tea. Similar flow charts can be used to describe the operation of telephone systems, library check-out routines, document preparation etc. Although work instructions can comprise an essential component of a documented quality assurance system, they are clearly distinct from QAPs.

All QAPs contain the same eight elements: a title; an amendment record; a statement of purpose; a list of associated documents; definitions, if required; an indication of responsibility; an expression of scope; and an explanation of method. A title, which is related to an ISO 9001 : 1994 section heading, indicates the nature of the procedure.

An amendment record allows a practice to keep track of procedural changes. Procedures should not be viewed as 'written in stone'; they are living documents which will require revision as systems are improved and the needs of a practice

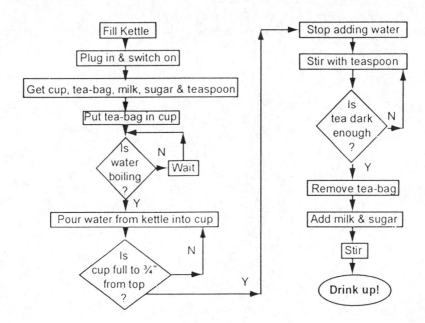

Figure 5.1   Work instruction

change. A statement of purpose, based on the appropriate section of the quality assurance manual, describes the policy objective of the procedure. Procedures should include a list of all associated documents including, for example, relevant QAM section numbers, Law Society practice rules, work instructions, forms etc. Definitions of unusual or confusing terms, if required, should be listed. The procedure must indicate who has responsibility for the various tasks covered including revision of the procedure itself. The scope of the procedure should be explained.

The procedure must contain an explanation of the method employed to meet the policy objective. Overall, the drafter of a procedure should be careful not to make it too complicated. Procedures written to encompass every possibility are usually overly constraining and frequently ignored. Methods and respective procedures should be modified as new needs are recognised and improvements for meeting those needs are developed. Regular reviews and audits help to keep procedures up to date with changes in method. The ultimate goal is continuous improvement which is fostered through constant feedback of information on how the system is working. This can best come from the users of the system.

The following example procedures cover the required sections of ISO 9001 : 1994. They describe one fictional firm's methods for meeting its quality objectives.

They are not intended to suggest that all practices must operate the same way. All practices are different and have their own unique circumstances and needs. Consequently, quality assurance procedures must be custom-tailored to each application.

HITCHCOCK, SIMPSON, HARGRAVE, COKE & LITTLETON
QUALITY ASSURANCE PROCEDURE 1 (QAP 1)

QUALITY SYSTEM AUDIT AND REVIEW

AMENDMENT RECORD

This procedure is a mandatory requirement and forms part of the approved documented quality system.

Alterations are not permitted without the prior approval of Mr R.T. Hitchcock.

Issue	Date	Approved	Summary of change

HITCHCOCK, SIMPSON, HARGRAVE, COKE & LITTLETON
QUALITY ASSURANCE PROCEDURE 1 (QAP 1)

QUALITY SYSTEM AUDIT AND REVIEW

1 PURPOSE

Quality audits and reviews are carried out to ensure that:

(a) Hitchcock, Simpson, Hargrave, Coke & Littleton's quality assurance system is effective in achieving and maintaining the levels required by ISO 9001 : 1994.

(b) Any weaknesses in the business operation are eliminated in order to improve quality and economic operation.

The purpose of audit is to verify whether quality activities comply with planned arrangements and to determine the current effectiveness of the quality system.

The purpose of management review is to ensure the documented quality system's continuing suitability and effectiveness.

2 ASSOCIATED DOCUMENTS

Hitchcock, Simpson, Hargrave, Coke & Littleton's Quality Assurance Manual, sections 2, 5, and 20.

3 RESPONSIBILITY

3.1 General

Mr R.T. Hitchcock has overall responsibility for the preparation and implementation of the Firm's quality audit plan, showing the timing of audits and reviews. He shall subcontract, to an appropriately qualified auditor, the preparation of an audit and review plan for approval, and subsequently ensure that all audits are carried out to the agreed plan in a timely and effective manner. The appointed auditor will carry out the agreed audits, prepare reports, recommend corrective actions and improvements to the system as necessary. He shall participate in quality assurance review team meetings as required.

3.2 Approval

Mr R.T. Hitchcock is responsible for approval of, and compliance with, the Audit Plan.

3.3   Control

Mr S.P. Littleton has responsibility for the issue and control of this procedure.

4   SCOPE

This procedure applies to all Hitchcock, Simpson, Hargrave, Coke & Littleton operations.

5   METHOD

5.1   Audit

5.1.1   Planning
All quality assurance documentation including the Quality Assurance Manual and procedures, and their operation, shall be audited over each 12 month period. The audits shall be planned by compiling a list of all items to be audited (see annex 1) and spreading the work evenly over the period in accordance with the status and importance of the activities.

5.1.2   Organisation
The auditor/s shall prepare, from the quality assurance documents applicable to the operation to be audited, a note of the quality assurance practices that should be in operation, and compile a checklist for the audit to be carried out

5.1.3   Implementation
An essential part of the audit is to confirm that all parts of the quality assurance system are being conscientiously applied by all staff; that they are aware of, and are using, the correct issues of procedures and instructions appropriate to their particular work, and are aware of their own particular contribution to quality. All staff are encouraged to make suggestions for improvement to the quality system.

The quality manual, procedures, work instructions and records shall be audited for:

(a)   effectiveness, adequacy and completeness,
(b)   updating for improved techniques and methods,
(c)   amendment considered necessary from experience in application.

All proposals for changes shall be put to the quality assurance review team for approval.

5.1.4   Documentation
A report shall be raised for each audit carried out (annex 2) showing the items covered, the findings, and the corrective actions (annex 3) required and taken. Audit reports shall be retained by the section for a period of three years.

5.2   Review

5.2.1   Planning
Reviews shall be planned to take place every three months (or more frequently as required), and shall be carried out by the quality assurance review team (Mr R.T. Hitchcock, Mr S.P. Littleton and Mrs R.A. Long), together with other staff required for particular topics.

5.2.2   Organisation and Implementation
The agenda should include the following items, together with any appropriate items from annex 4, as appropriate:

(a)   quality audit results — progress to plan, reports, proposals for improvement, review of previous corrective actions,

(b)   quality system considerations — policy and objectives continuing suitability and effectiveness in the light of business, people and technological changes.

5.2.3   Records
Each meeting shall be minuted and the minutes filed and retained for a period of three years.

HITCHCOCK, SIMPSON, HARGRAVE, COKE & LITTLETON
ANNEX 1 TO QAP 1
AUDIT PLAN

Hitchcock, Simpson, Hargrave, Coke & Littleton
Quality Assurance Audit Plan 1994
Issue .... Page ...... of ....

No.	Planned audit	Auditor/s	J	F	M	A	M	J	J	A	S	O	N	D

Originator .... Date ....

Key:

☐ Audit planned

■ Audit completed: no deficiencies

○ Fix date for deficiencies

Ⓔ Follow-up unsatisfactory: escalate

☐------☐ Programme slip and recovery

▨ Deficiencies found and reported

○------○ Fix date slip and recovery

● Deficiencies fixed: completed

HITCHCOCK, SIMPSON, HARGRAVE, COKE & LITTLETON
ANNEX 2 TO QAP 1
AUDIT REPORT FORM

Hitchcock, Simpson, Hargrave, Coke & Littleton: AUDIT REPORT

Report Number:......................................
 Date of Audit:.......................................
 	
 Areas and/or procedures audited:
         1...
         2...
         3...
         4...
         5...
 Staff contacted:
 	
 Applicable documents and issue numbers:
 	
 Audited by:..

SUMMARY OF FINDINGS:
List of corrective action requests (CARs) made, and persons responsible for action:
Signed:..Date:.........................

HITCHCOCK, SIMPSON, HARGRAVE, COKE & LITTLETON
ANNEX 3 TO QAP 1
CORRECTIVE ACTION REQUEST (CAR) FORM

Hitchcock, Simpson, Hargrave, Coke & Littleton

CORRECTIVE ACTION REQUEST (CAR) FORM

Audit report number:.................Date carried out:......................
Subject of audit:
Name of auditor..........................
1   Discrepancy found during audit: Signed:...Date............................
2   Action recommended: Signed...Date............................
3   Action taken: Signed...Date............................
4   Review of action taken: Signed...Date............................

HITCHCOCK, SIMPSON, HARGRAVE, COKE & LITTLETON
ANNEX 4 TO QAP 1
REVIEW: NOTES FOR GUIDANCE

Effective operation
Is the QA system generally being followed and working smoothly?

Corrective action
Have corrective actions approved at previous meetings proved effective?

Economy
The application of the QA system should have significant economic gains, for example, in the reduction of wasted time and 'firefighting', improvements in client communications, subcontractor performance and in methods generally.
    Are these benefits being realised?
    Is any part of the system being excessively applied thereby causing unnecessary expenditure?
    Is some of the work of the section uneconomic due to excessive complexity or some other reason?
    Can the operation be improved by better information, better systems, better suppliers, better client liaison, etc?

Planning and management
Is work planning adequate and effective?
    Have there been any problems due to deficiencies in planning, progressing and management?

Processes
Have any problems or defects been attributed to shortcomings in work procedures or equipment?
    Have improvements been made?
    Are the procedures acceptable and understood?
    Are they efficiently operated?

Documentation control
Have all outstanding changes been implemented?
    Has obsolete documentation been withdrawn?

Records
Are records being maintained? Any problems?

Stock control
Confirm stock and stores satisfactory operation.

Staff training
Check the effectiveness of the training procedures and arrange for further training as necessary.

Client liaison
Has cooperation with clients been satisfactory?
   Have there been any client complaints?

Project control
Where dates have been promised, are they being met?

HITCHCOCK, SIMPSON, HARGRAVE, COKE & LITTLETON
ANNEX 5 TO QAP 1
GUIDANCE LIST FOR AUDIT

Documentation
Is all documentation in place and controlled?
 Issue numbered and dated?
 Approved by the correct authority?
 Available in areas where needed?
 Clearly written, understood and acceptable to users?
 Obsolete copies removed?

Procedures
Do all the activities covered by ISO 9001 have procedures?
 Are these procedures being applied correctly?
 Have all previous corrective actions been carried out?

Planning
Have instructions been taken and recorded in case files?
 Has a work plan been drawn up before starting work?

Records
Are there records of essential quality assurance activities?
 Are they analysed and used for management action?
 Are there satisfactory means of storage and retrieval?

Purchasing
Is the system of subcontractor selection effective?
 Do purchasing documents clearly describe requirements?
 Is verification of services received properly controlled?

Training
Are training arrangements satisfactory?

HITCHCOCK, SIMPSON, HARGRAVE, COKE & LITTLETON
QUALITY ASSURANCE PROCEDURE 2 (QAP 2)

INSTRUCTION REVIEW

AMENDMENT RECORD

This procedure is a mandatory requirement and forms part of the approved documented quality system.

Alterations are not permitted without the prior approval of Mr R.T. Hitchcock.

Issue	Date	Approved	Summary of change

HITCHCOCK, SIMPSON, HARGRAVE, COKE & LITTLETON
QUALITY ASSURANCE PROCEDURE 2 (QAP 2)

INSTRUCTION REVIEW

1 PURPOSE

Instruction review is carried out in order to ensure that all client instructions are adequately defined and documented, that any requirements differing from any earlier tender, quotation or understanding of the client's needs are resolved and that the Firm is capable of meeting contractual requirements.

2 ASSOCIATED DOCUMENTS

Hitchcock, Simpson, Hargrave, Coke & Littleton Quality Assurance Manual, section 6.

3 RESPONSIBILITY

Mr R.T. Hitchcock has ultimate responsibility, and all fee-earners have day-to-day responsibility, for instruction review at Hitchcock, Simpson, Hargrave, Coke & Littleton.

Mr S.P. Littleton is responsible for the issue and control of this procedure.

4 SCOPE

This procedure applies to all client matters undertaken by Hitchcock, Simpson, Hargrave, Coke & Littleton.

5 METHOD

5.1 Background

Work is carried out by Hitchcock, Simpson, Hargrave, Coke & Littleton on behalf of corporate clients. Occasionally, work is carried out on a *pro bono* basis on behalf of individual clients.

Most client instructions are received by Hitchcock, Simpson, Hargrave, Coke & Littleton by telephone. Occasionally, client instructions are received in writing.

Details of individual matters to be carried out (including quality requirements, client instructions, deadlines and budget) are specified in the telephoned or written instructions.

Hourly rates for fee-earners are periodically set by the Firm's partners and are sometimes negotiated with clients.

5.2 Review

All client instructions (and amendments to instructions) received by Hitchcock, Simpson, Hargrave, Coke & Littleton, whether written or verbal, are immediately reviewed for the clear definition of client requirements and the Firm's ability to meet them. Any uncertainties, ambiguities or discrepancies are resolved by direct contact with the client and the instruction is suitably amended. Where needed by the client, specialised knowledge and experience are offered by the Firm for the client's guidance.

Special requirements (such as deadline, budget restriction, workload and the need for outside counsel) are all checked during the review.

5.3 Review completion

On completion of the review, the fee-earner assigned to handle the matter informs the client in writing of his or her understanding of the client's requirements and of his or her course of action in providing legal representation. Duplicates of all correspondence are kept in a file which is opened by the assigned fee-earner. The file is labelled with client information including: client number, matter number, minute reference and date. The opening of a file is recorded on the Firm's computer.

6   RECORDS

Records of reviews on the above documentation are retained for five years or as may be required by contract.

HITCHCOCK, SIMPSON, HARGRAVE, COKE & LITTLETON
QUALITY ASSURANCE PROCEDURE 3 (QAP 3)

PROJECT CONTROL

AMENDMENT RECORD

This procedure is a mandatory requirement and forms part of the approved documented quality system.

Alterations are not permitted without the prior approval of Mr R.T. Hitchcock.

Issue	Date	Approved	Summary of change

HITCHCOCK, SIMPSON, HARGRAVE, COKE & LITTLETON
QUALITY ASSURANCE PROCEDURE 3 (QAP3)

PROJECT CONTROL

1 PURPOSE

Project control is carried out to control and verify all aspects of legal work undertaken by Hitchcock, Simpson, Hargrave, Coke & Littleton to ensure that contractual requirements are met. All legal work undertaken is planned through to completion or disposal.

2 ASSOCIATED DOCUMENTS

Hitchcock, Simpson, Hargrave, Coke & Littleton Quality Assurance Manual, section 7.

3 RESPONSIBILITY

Mr R.T. Hitchcock has ultimate responsibility, and all fee-earners have day-to-day responsibility, for Project Control in Hitchcock, Simpson, Hargrave, Coke & Littleton.

Mr S.P. Littleton is responsible for the issue and control of this procedure.

4 SCOPE

This procedure applies to all legal work undertaken by Hitchcock, Simpson, Hargrave, Coke & Littleton.

5 METHOD

5.1 Background

Work is carried out by Hitchcock, Simpson, Hargrave, Coke & Littleton on behalf of corporate clients. Occasionally, work is carried out on a *pro bono* basis on behalf of individuals.

Hourly rates for fee earners are periodically determined by the Firm's partners and are occasionally negotiated with clients. Details of individual matters to be carried out (including quality requirements, client instructions, deadlines and budget) are specified in the written or telephoned instructions.

5.2 Project control

Client instructions are received by Hitchcock, Simpson, Hargrave, Coke & Littleton in the form of memoranda, by telephone or in writing. In assigning work to fee-earners, consideration is given to make sure that the fee-earner handling the matter has had the appropriate training and experience for dealing with the type of matter, that no conflict of interests exist and has the resources and time to handle the matter satisfactorily to conclusion. The fee-earner who is assigned work identifies the client's requirements and resolves with the client any inadequacies or discrepancies. Once resolved, he or she confirms his or her understanding to the client in writing of the work required and of the facts as presented by the client. This written statement includes the fee-earner's understanding of any client or legally imposed deadline, any financial restrictions and the client's desired result.

The fee-earner prepares quality plans [an example is shown in annex 1] for each matter undertaken stating how it should be progressed, who is responsible for each aspect of it, what information, *matériel*, witnesses and services will need to be acquired for completion of the case either from the client or from other sources. These quality plans are placed in the matter file. In the case of routine matters, the fee-earner prepares blanket quality plans which are kept with the matter records they relate to. All quality plans are updated to reflect any significant plan changes which occur as work on the matter evolves. The update includes an explanation for the change. The client's consent is obtained and documented for any significant plan changes.

The fee-earner records on time cards: the time spent working on a matter, a description of the type of work done, a description of progress made in relation to the quality plan and client, matter and fee-earner identification information. These time cards are stored in reverse date order in the relevant matter file.

All court or hearing dates are recorded on a central day planner.

The quality plan, correspondence and documents in a file, time-cards and the central day planner permit the progress of a matter to be subject to verification by Firm management to ensure that progress has been made which will achieve the desired result and to ensure that no important point has been missed.

The fee-earner regularly consults with other fee-earners responsible for the same matter, especially at critical stages.

HITCHCOCK, SIMPSON, HARGRAVE, COKE & LITTLETON
ANNEX 1 TO QAP 3

EXAMPLE QUALITY PLAN (*Courtesy of Mr R. Holman.*)

Quality Plan for drafting an Assured Shorthold Tenancy Lease

1   Terms of reference.
2   Research law:

   (a)   Landlord and Tenant Act 1954.
   (b)   Landlord and Tenant Act 1985.
   (c)   Housing Act 1988.

3   Review facts with client:

   (a)   Description of the property and ownership.
   (b)   Length of tenancy and cost.
   (c)   What is the landlord liable for?
   (d)   What is the tenant liable for?
   (e)   Restrictions on usage.
   (f)   Service of prescribed notice.

4   Draft Tenancy Agreement and Prescribed Notice.

5   Review Tenancy Agreement:

   (a)   Check for mistakes.
   (b)   Check for compliance with legal requirements.

6   Result:

   (a)   Confirm with client that tenancy agreement fulfils client's needs.
   (b)   Deliver tenancy agreement to client for signature.
   (c)   Serve prescribed notice on tenant.
   (d)   Complete tenancy agreement and prescribed notice.
   (e)   Advise client and invoice.

HITCHCOCK, SIMPSON, HARGRAVE, COKE & LITTLETON
QUALITY ASSURANCE PROCEDURE 4 (QAP 4)

QUALITY DOCUMENT CONTROL

AMENDMENT RECORD

This procedure is a mandatory requirement and forms part of the approved documented quality system.

Alterations are not permitted without the prior approval of Mr R.T. Hitchcock.

Issue	Date	Approved	Summary of change

HITCHCOCK, SIMPSON, HARGRAVE, COKE & LITTLETON
QUALITY ASSURANCE PROCEDURE 4 (QAP 4)

QUALITY DOCUMENT CONTROL

1   PURPOSE

Quality document control is carried out in order to ensure that all documents and data relating to quality assurance and the practice of law are reviewed and approved for adequacy by authorised personnel prior to issue, that the pertinent issues of relevant documents are available where their absence would adversely affect quality, and that obsolete documents are promptly removed from all points of issue or use.

2   ASSOCIATED DOCUMENTS

Hitchcock, Simpson, Hargrave, Coke & Littleton's Quality Assurance Manual, section 8.

3   DEFINITIONS

Quality plan: A plan for the conduct of specific items of professional work handled by the section, setting out the quality controls, resources and activities relating to that work item.

4   RESPONSIBILITY

Mr R.T. Hitchcock is responsible for the authorisation, and distribution control, of the Quality Assurance Manual and supporting quality assurance procedures.

Mr S.P. Littleton is responsible for the preparation, retention, and distribution of the Quality Assurance Manual and supporting quality assurance procedures to Mr Hitchcock's requirements.

Fee-earners are responsible for the authorisation, and distribution control, of all documents relevant to their practice of law.

Support staff are responsible for the preparation, retention, and distribution of documents relevant to the Firm's practice in accordance with instructions from fee-earners.

5   SCOPE

This procedure applies to all documents and data required for quality assurance at Hitchcock, Simpson, Hargrave, Coke & Littleton including:

    (a)   the Quality Assurance Manual,
    (b)   Quality Assurance Procedures,
    (c)   Quality plans,

and to all documents and data required for the practice of law including:

    (a)   files,
    (b)   correspondence,
    (d)   client-supplied documents.

6   METHOD

6.1   Review

All Hitchcock, Simpson, Hargrave, Coke & Littleton's quality assurance and legal practice documents shall be reviewed by the originator for correctness and adequacy on completion.

6.2   Authorisation

Once checked as correct, quality assurance documents shall be authorised for use by Mr. R.T. Hitchcock (or another authorised person in his absence) and shall be allocated a Hitchcock, Simpson, Hargrave, Coke & Littleton reference, issue number and issue date.

Any changes to quality assurance documents shall be approved by Mr. Hitchcock or another authorised person in his absence, and shall be implemented by document reissue as detailed in 6.7 below.

6.3   Client documents

Any documents provided by the client with an instruction shall be reviewed on receipt as part of instruction review, to ensure that they are correct and adequate.

Client changes to their instructions shall be confirmed to the client in writing and a copy of said confirmation placed in the relevant file.

6.4   Distribution

All quality assurance manuals, procedures and instructions shall be issued as necessary to the locations concerned with the particular subject. Staff shall be instructed in the quality assurance documents applying to their work. The quality assurance documents shall be readily available for reference in every instance where their absence might adversely affect quality. Copies of these documents are available to all those who need them to carry out their work.

6.5 Additional copies

Additional copies of quality assurance documents shall be provided as required, by Mr. S.P. Littleton; under no circumstances is it permitted for additional copies to be obtained from any uncontrolled duplication process.

6.6 Superseded documents

Recipients of documents shall ensure that, normally, all superseded documents and instructions are destroyed. If it is necessary to retain copies for reference or historical purposes, they shall be clearly marked 'Superseded — for information only'.

6.7 Change control

Changes to quality assurance documents shall be implemented by increment in issue number and date, and document reissue. The quality assurance documents shall be reissued with amendment records as follows:

(a) QA manual — by pages until a complete reissue is required (annex 1).

(b) QA procedures — a complete reissue for each change (annex 2).

(c) All other quality assurance documents — a complete reissue for each change, with the reasons for change shown either on a note as shown in annex 2 or included in the document (e.g., for instruction confirmation changes).

6.8 Records

A master record shall be made and maintained of all changes to, and the issue status of, all quality assurance and documentation. A register shall be kept of all controlled quality assurance manuals in circulation. A standard distribution list shall be used for all other controlled documents.

A master record shall be made and maintained of all files, deeds, and valuable client-supplied documents, materials and funds. A distribution list shall be used for these files, deeds, and valuable client-supplied documents, materials and funds.

HITCHCOCK, SIMPSON, HARGRAVE, COKE & LITTLETON
ANNEX 1 TO QAP 4
QUALITY MANUAL AMENDMENT RECORD

Amendment number	Section number	Page number	Issue number	Date	Authorisation

HITCHCOCK, SIMPSON, HARGRAVE, COKE & LITTLETON
ANNEX 2 TO QAP 4

QUALITY ASSURANCE PROCEDURES AMENDMENT RECORD

Issue	Date	Approved	Summary of Change

HITCHCOCK, SIMPSON, HARGRAVE, COKE & LITTLETON
QUALITY ASSURANCE PROCEDURE 5 (QAP 5)

PURCHASING

AMENDMENT RECORD

This procedure is a mandatory requirement and forms part of the approved documented quality system.

Alterations are not permitted without the prior approval of Mr R.T. Hitchcock.

Issue	Date	Approved	Summary of change

HITCHCOCK, SIMPSON, HARGRAVE, COKE & LITTLETON
QUALITY ASSURANCE PROCEDURE 5 (QAP 5)

PURCHASING

1 PURPOSE

The purpose of this procedure is to ensure the procurement of bought-out items and services of the required quality at competitive prices by the planned delivery dates.

2 ASSOCIATED DOCUMENTS

Hitchcock, Simpson, Hargrave, Coke & Littleton's Quality Assurance Manual, section 8.

3 DEFINITIONS

Delivery: completion or disposal of a matter.

Purchasing: the purchase of products or services from suppliers/subcontractors.

Quality: 'the totality of features and characteristics of a product or service that bear on its ability to satisfy stated or implied needs' (ISO 8402). The concept of quality is appropriately expressed as 'fitness for purpose', which here is taken to include considerations of cost-effectiveness and timeliness.

Supplier (ISO 9001:1994 term: subcontractor): any business or individual from whom the Firm purchases or obtains materials or skills, ranging from suppliers of items such as computers or of such skills as training and consultancy, including barristers and technical experts whose advice and opinions are used in providing the Firm's legal services.

4 RESPONSIBILITY

4.1 Signatories

The authorised signatories of Hitchcock, Simpson, Hargrave, Coke & Littleton's purchase orders are:

Mr R.T. Hitchcock
Mr E.B. Simpson
Mrs R.A. Long (for amounts under £500)

They are responsible for the application of this procedure and for the review and approval of purchasing documents for adequacy of specified requirements prior to release.

4.2   Control

Mr R.T. Hitchcock is responsible for the issue and control of this procedure, and for the maintenance of a register of approved suppliers.

5   SCOPE

This procedure applies to all Hitchcock, Simpson, Hargrave, Coke & Littleton's operations.

6   METHOD

6.1   Selection of suppliers

Suitable suppliers appropriate to the requirements shall be selected from the register of approved suppliers of goods and services. This register shall be compiled on the basis of the proven ability of suppliers to meet the required standards of quality, price and delivery.

Where it is necessary to consider suppliers not on the list, assessment shall be carried out as appropriate to the requirement by the authorities defined in 3 above.

Given the nature of legal work, it is seldom possible to impose purchase controls over suppliers of legal services. Consequently, the main purchase control is the determination whether or not to use the supplier again.

6.2   Purchase documents

6.2.1   Ordering data
Purchase documents shall state:

  (a)   the Hitchcock, Simpson, Hargrave, Coke & Littleton order number,
  (b)   the name of the supplier,
  (c)   the date of order,
  (d)   the supplier's quotation reference and quoted price (where applicable),
  (e)   a full description of the items or services ordered, together with the quantity, duration, or other definition of supply,
  (f)   the delivery date promised or required,
  (g)   any required reference to contract requirements, technical and/or legal requirements where applicable, and any applicable quality specification.

6.2.2 Amendments

All amendments to orders shall be confirmed in writing. Where verbal changes are made for reasons of urgency, an amendment shall be issued, marked 'Confirmation of verbal amendment — do not duplicate', by the authorised signatory making the change.

6.3 Progress

Orders shall be monitored as necessary to confirm and expedite delivery.

6.4 Consultation

Where applicable to a particular matter, visits to and consultation with the supplier may be agreed with the client.

HITCHCOCK, SIMPSON, HARGRAVE, COKE & LITTLETON
ANNEX 1 TO QAP 4
PURCHASE ORDER

Hitchcock, Simpson, Hargrave, Coke & Littleton

Hitchcock House
46 High Street
London SW1 4GH   (Tel. 0171-555-1212) (Fax 0171-555-1213)

PURCHASE ORDER

The following number must appear on all related correspondence, shipping papers, and invoices:
P.O. NUMBER: 95-00167

To:
    Gordon Walker & Associates
    8 Chester Place
    Mutley
    Plymouth PL4 6ET

Ship To:
    NA

P.O. DATE	REQUISITIONER	SHIP VIA	F.O.B. POINT	TERMS
15/3/95	Hargrave	NA	NA	30 Days

QTY	UNIT	DESCRIPTION	UNIT PRICE	TOTAL
15	Days	quality assurance consultancy to prepare a documented quality system in conformance with ISO 9001:1994, introduce firm to concepts of quality assurance, and assist in implementing quality assurance plan; all in accordance with your quotation, terms of reference and project plan ref: w\q\l dated 12/3/95.	£1,000.00	£15,000.00
		SUBTOTAL		£15,000.00
		VAT		£2,625.00
		SHIPPING & HANDLING		
		OTHER		
		TOTAL		£17,625.00

1. Please send two copies of your invoice.

2. Enter this order in accordance with the prices, terms, delivery method, and specifications listed above.

3. Please notify us immediately if you are unable to comply as specified.

4. Send all correspondence to:
    Hitchcock, Simpson, Hargrave, Coke & Littleton
    Hitchcock House
    46 High Street
    London SW1 4GH
    (Tel. 0171-555-1212) (Fax 0171-555-1213)

Authorized by _____   Date _____

HITCHCOCK, SIMPSON, HARGRAVE, COKE & LITTLETON
QUALITY ASSURANCE PROCEDURE 6 (QAP 6)

CLIENT SUPPLIED MATERIAL

AMENDMENT RECORD

This procedure is a mandatory requirement and forms part of the approved documented quality system.

Alterations are not permitted without the prior approval of Mr R.T. Hitchcock.

Issue	Date	Approved	Summary of change

HITCHCOCK, SIMPSON, HARGRAVE, COKE & LITTLETON
QUALITY ASSURANCE PROCEDURE 6 (QAP 6)

CLIENT-SUPPLIED MATERIAL

1 PURPOSE

The purpose of this procedure is to control material supplied by clients, and safeguard it against loss, damage or deterioration.

2 ASSOCIATED DOCUMENTS

Hitchcock, Simpson, Hargrave, Coke & Littleton's Quality Assurance Manual, section 10.

Quality Assurance Procedure 9 — Verification of Work and Verification Monitoring.

3 RESPONSIBILITY

Mr R.T. Hitchcock is responsible for the authorisation, and distribution control, of the Quality Assurance Manual and supporting quality assurance procedures.

Mr S.P. Littleton is responsible for the preparation, retention and distribution of the Quality Assurance Manual and supporting quality assurance procedures to Mr. Hitchcock's requirements.

Each fee-earner is responsible for implementing this procedure with regard to work undertaken. All individuals are responsible for the overall control and preservation of client-supplied material which is in their safekeeping.

4 SCOPE

This procedure applies to all client-supplied material at Hitchcock, Simpson, Hargrave, Coke & Littleton, and may include, for example, deeds, plans, funds and documents. It also applies to all information and services that are used in providing legal services, including experts' reports and barristers' opinions.

5 METHOD

5.1 Inspection

Goods inward inspection shall be carried out on any material, information or documentation of service which is received by Hitchcock, Simpson, Hargrave, Coke & Littleton directly in accordance with the verification of work procedure

(QAP 9) to ensure that the material, information or service correspond with the description referred to in the accompanying documentation.

Inspection shall be carried out by the fee-earner concerned (or by his or her nominee) on any material supplied by a client or client's agent or by the supplier of information and services that are used in providing legal services. On receipt, all damage, discrepancies, and material, information and services which are unfit for purpose shall be reported to the client and/or provider of the information or service, immediately.

5.2 Verification

During the negotiation for representation, the requirement and extent of any checking by Hitchcock, Simpson, Hargrave, Coke & Littleton to verify client-supplied documents or procedures and information and services that are used in providing legal services shall be agreed and recorded. This shall be confirmed in the quality plan, where appropriate, with details of the verification method.

Such verification shall not absolve the client or information or service provider of the responsibility to provide acceptable documents, information, service or material as agreed.

Where information is supplied by the client without warranty (and verification of this by Hitchcock, Simpson, Hargrave, Coke & Littleton is outside the terms of reference) then these items shall be identified and the significance of possible inaccuracies or omissions reported to the client and/or information or service provider.

5.3 Identification

All material belonging to a client shall be clearly identified as such throughout all stages of storage or use. All information and services provided from sources outside Hitchcock, Simpson, Hargrave, Coke & Littleton shall be clearly identified as such throughout all stages of storage or use.

5.4 Storage and maintenance

Client-supplied material shall be stored in an appropriate manner to ensure security and preservation whilst in the safe keeping of Hitchcock, Simpson, Hargrave, Coke & Littleton. This shall be the subject of liaison with the client if necessary.

5.5 Usage

Proper instructions shall be given, where required, for the safe and proper usage of client-supplied material, avoiding damage and deterioration.

5.6 Services

If any work instruction should include services to be provided by the client or other party (e.g., barrister, expert), these services shall be subject to agreed control procedures to maintain the quality standard of the finished output.

5.7 Reporting

Any client-supplied material that is lost, damaged or otherwise rendered unsuitable for use whilst in Hitchcock, Simpson, Hargrave, Coke & Littleton's possession shall be reported to the client.

5.8 Records

Records shall be maintained of client-supplied material held by Hitchcock, Simpson, Hargrave, Coke & Littleton. Records shall be maintained for five years or as may be required by law.

HITCHCOCK, SIMPSON, HARGRAVE, COKE & LITTLETON
QUALITY ASSURANCE PROCEDURE 7 (QAP 7)

IDENTIFICATION AND TRACEABILITY

AMENDMENT RECORD

This procedure is a mandatory requirement and forms part of the approved documented quality system.

Alterations are not permitted without the prior approval of Mr R.T. Hitchcock.

Issue	Date	Approved	Summary of change

HITCHCOCK, SIMPSON, HARGRAVE, COKE & LITTLETON
QUALITY ASSURANCE PROCEDURE 7 (QAP 7)

IDENTIFICATION AND TRACEABILITY

1 PURPOSE

The purpose of this procedure is to define the requirements for identification and traceability for services provided by Hitchcock, Simpson, Hargrave, Coke & Littleton.

2 ASSOCIATED DOCUMENTS

Hitchcock, Simpson, Hargrave, Coke & Littleton's Quality Assurance Manual, section 11.
QAP 2, Instruction Review.

3 RESPONSIBILITY

Mr R.T. Hitchcock is responsible for the authorisation, and distribution control, of the Quality Assurance Manual and supporting quality assurance procedures.

Mr S.P. Littleton is responsible for the preparation, retention, and distribution of the Quality Assurance Manual and supporting quality assurance procedures to Mr Hitchcock's requirements.

Fee earners have overall responsibility for meeting and maintaining the required identification and traceability requirements on work in progress, completed work they are responsible for and services or material purchased with regard to a case or matter, and for ensuring that adequate records are kept.

Mr. R.T. Hitchcock and his support staff subordinates have responsibility for meeting and maintaining the required identification and traceability requirements with regard to non-case or matter-related purchasing.

4 SCOPE

This procedure applies to all work and purchases undertaken by Hitchcock, Simpson, Hargrave, Coke & Littleton.

5 METHOD

5.1 Reference system

Hitchcock, Simpson, Hargrave, Coke & Littleton shall maintain a case reference system that ensures that each individual case or matter has a unique reference number. This system shall allow Hitchcock, Simpson, Hargrave, Coke & Littleton to identify and trace, at all times, all information, correspondence, documents and material relating to a case or matter. Identification and traceability requirements for cases or matters are generally universal with regard to all work carried out by Hitchcock, Simpson, Hargrave, Coke & Littleton. These requirements are indicated herein. Any special identification and traceability requirements for a particular case or matter are determined (at the time of instruction review) on receipt in Hitchcock, Simpson, Hargrave, Coke & Littleton of instructions.

5.1.1 Receiving procedure

Upon receipt of any instruction, a case file shall be created that includes a label which indicates: the type of matter, client address, opposing party, minute reference, date, fee earner assigned and a reference code. The existence of the case file shall be recorded on computer.

All information, correspondence, documents and material relating to a case shall be identified and placed in the appropriate case file. Where information is communicated orally, the information shall be reduced to writing and placed in the appropriate case file. Where documents and material relating to a case are too large to place in a file, a note shall be placed in the file indicating the section's receipt of the documents or material and indicating where they are stored.

5.1.2 Segregation
All incoming information, correspondence, documents and material relating to a case awaiting identification shall be retained separately from previously identified items.

5.1.3 Accepted information, correspondence, documents and material relating to a case and indication of identification
Indication that items have passed inward identification shall be made by inspection records on the incoming documentation or by indicating said information in the appropriate case file.

All items that have passed identification shall be transferred to the appropriate case file or to the vault without delay.

5.2 Stage identification and traceability

5.2.1 Stages
At each stage of work in progress, copies of work completed shall be placed in the appropriate case file. When work product supersedes previous work product, the previous work product should be marked accordingly (e.g., a prior draft of a contract should be marked 'Superseded').

5.2.2 Subcontract identification and traceability

The responsibility for maintaining a case reference system with regard to work which is subcontracted shall lie with the subcontractor. This shall be specified in the relevant Hitchcock, Simpson, Hargrave, Coke & Littleton purchase order, and all the necessary case references shall be provided with the purchase order.

5.3 Final identification and traceability

Files for completed matters or cases shall be adequately stored and documented for the period of time required by law.

5.4 Purchases

Material or record of services received against Hitchcock, Simpson, Hargrave, Coke & Littleton purchase orders shall be related to the order upon receipt in Hitchcock, Simpson, Hargrave, Coke & Littleton. On receipt in the section, the material or record of services shall be identified, and dealt with as shown above in 5.1.

5.4.1 Identification

Any subcontracted work shall have the identification retained to the extent of being able to refer back to the subcontractors in the event of quality problems. Identification shall be retained throughout the subcontract process.

5.4.2 Stock usage

Where applicable, stock identification of office supplies shall be used to ensure stock rotation (oldest material to be used first) and monitoring of shelf life. Stocks past their expiry date or otherwise unsuitable for use shall be disposed of.

5.4.3 Records

Records are required to the extent that purchased services and material are identifiable and traceable to source should subsequent quality problems arise. Records shall be retained for one year from completion of the work or as may be required by contract or law.

HITCHCOCK, SIMPSON, HARGRAVE, COKE & LITTLETON
QUALITY ASSURANCE PROCEDURE 8 (QAP 8)

WORK MONITORING

AMENDMENT RECORD

This procedure is a mandatory requirement and forms part of the approved documented quality system.

Alterations are not permitted without the prior approval of Mr R.T. Hitchcock.

Issue	Date	Approved	Summary of change

HITCHCOCK, SIMPSON, HARGRAVE, COKE & LITTLETON
QUALITY ASSURANCE PROCEDURE 8 (QAP 8)

WORK MONITORING

1 PURPOSE

The purpose of this procedure is to ensure that work which directly affects quality
is carried out under controlled conditions so as to meet the required performance
and quality standards.

2 ASSOCIATED DOCUMENTS

Hitchcock, Simpson, Hargrave, Coke & Littleton Quality Assurance Manual,
section 12.
   QAP 2, Instruction Review.

3 RESPONSIBILITY

Mr R.T. Hitchcock is responsible for the authorisation, and distribution control, of
the Quality Assurance Manual and supporting quality assurance procedures.
   Mr S.P. Littleton is responsible for the preparation, retention, and distribution of
the Quality Assurance Manual and supporting quality assurance procedures to Mr
Hitchcock's requirements.
   Fee-earners have overall responsibility for ensuring that work monitoring
procedures are adhered to with reference to cases or matters to which they have
been assigned.

4 SCOPE

This procedure applies to all work undertaken by Hitchcock, Simpson, Hargrave,
Coke & Littleton.

5 METHOD

5.1 Allocation of work

On receipt of work instructions, Mr Hitchcock, Mr Simpson, Mr Hargrave, Mr
Coke or Mr Littleton assign work to fee earners or sub-contractors taking into
consideration their expertise, qualifications, workload and ability to meet quality
standards.

5.2 Planning

A quality plan shall be drawn up, and special work identified, where required. All work shall be planned and scheduled in an economic manner, taking account of: required completion dates, staff or subcontractor resources, staff or subcontractor qualifications, cost of staff or subcontractor and subcontractor's availability, together with any requirements for further training.

If a work instruction involves an area of work beyond the Hitchcock, Simpson, Hargrave, Coke & Littleton's experience or ability to handle because of workload or lack of resources, Mr R.T. Hitchcock will consult the billing partner as to how the work is to be carried out and to resolve the quality assurance requirements. For large or complex work instructions, a client representative may be invited to join in the consultation if appropriate.

5.3 Purchasing

Fee-earners shall ensure that, so far as can reasonably be foreseen, all documents, material and services (e.g., deeds, exhibits, expert witnesses, barristers) are available to meet the quality plan requirements, and that the quality plan reflects these needs. Forward ordering procedures shall be applied where appropriate.

5.4 Documentation

All work shall be carried out to the quality plan appropriate to the work instruction. No work may be carried out without an appropriate reference, and work undertaken or services used shall be recorded in the case or matter file on completion of the work.

Before work is started, the availability and adequacy of documentation necessary to the case or matter (e.g., deeds, plans and contracts) shall be checked.

5.5 Progress

Work progress shall be regularly reviewed by Mr R.T. Hitchcock in conjunction with other staff as necessary, at intervals determined by the work load and urgency of clients' requirements. A vacation and absenteeism schedule shall be maintained so that Mr Littleton can ensure that appropriate progress on a matter is made even when any member of staff is absent.

Clients shall be advised regularly on the progress of matters. Each file shall include the date of last client contact.

All incoming correspondence shall be opened and prioritised immediately, to determine which requires immediate action.

HITCHCOCK, SIMPSON, HARGRAVE, COKE & LITTLETON
QUALITY ASSURANCE PROCEDURE 9 (QAP 9)

VERIFICATION OF WORK

AMENDMENT RECORD

This procedure is a mandatory requirement and forms part of the approved documented quality system.

Alterations are not permitted without the prior approval of Mr R.T. Hitchcock.

Issue	Date	Approved	Summary of change

HITCHCOCK, SIMPSON, HARGRAVE, COKE & LITTLETON
QUALITY ASSURANCE PROCEDURE 9 (QAP 9)

VERIFICATION OF WORK

1 PURPOSE

The purpose of this procedure is to ensure that work and material conform to specified requirements.

2 ASSOCIATED DOCUMENTS

Hitchcock, Simpson, Hargrave, Coke & Littleton Quality Assurance Manual, sections 13 and 15.

3 RESPONSIBILITY

Mr R.T. Hitchcock is responsible for the authorisation, and distribution control, of the Quality Assurance Manual and supporting quality assurance procedures.

Mr S.P. Littleton is responsible for the preparation, retention, and distribution of the Quality Assurance Manual and supporting quality assurance procedures to Mr Hitchcock's requirements.

Fee-earners are responsible for ensuring that adequate verification of work arrangements and instructions exist with regard to work they are responsible for, and that these requirements are understood and implemented.

Every individual is responsible for ensuring that any required work verification is carried out before work or material under his or her control is released to another.

4 SCOPE

This procedure applies to all work undertaken by Hitchcock, Simpson, Hargrave, Coke & Littleton.

5 METHOD

5.1 Inward Inspection

Hitchcock, Simpson, Hargrave, Coke & Littleton shall maintain a system for verifying all work including work supplied by subcontractors.

5.1.1 Receiving procedure

The condition of all material, and difficult-to-replace documents, pertaining to a case (e.g., physical exhibits, plans, deeds etc.) shall be checked prior to receipt. All damage and discrepancies shall be notified to the carrier and, where appropriate, the client immediately.

All information and services that are used in providing legal services, including experts' reports and barristers' opinions, shall be inspected by the fee-earner who has responsibility for the case or matter to determine whether the information or services meets case or matter requirements.

5.1.2 Segregation

All incoming material, difficult-to-replace documents, reports and opinions awaiting inspection shall be retained separately from previously inspected items.

5.1.3 Accepted material, difficult-to-replace documents, reports and opinions and indication of inspection

Indication that items have passed inward inspection shall be noted in the relevant case or matter file.

All items that have passed inspection shall be transferred to the appropriate case file or to the vault without delay.

5.1.4 Rejected material, difficult-to-replace documents, reports and opinions

Material, difficult-to-replace documents, reports and opinions which have been rejected at inward inspection shall be clearly defined as 'REJECTED' and shall have paperwork describing the reasons for non-acceptance attached. Rejected material, difficult-to-replace documents, reports and opinions shall be brought to the attention of the issuing party without delay.

5.2 Stage and final inspection

5.2.1 Work in progress

At each stage of work in progress, work shall be inspected to determine whether case or matter requirements are being met.

5.2.2 Inspection

Normal inspection consists of the application of the knowledge and experience of the individual carrying out the work, covering compliance with requirements.

5.2.3 Stage inspection and testing

As the work proceeds, work product shall be visually inspected by the individual carrying out the work to ensure that it conforms to any instructions or requirements, as appropriate. Any work product set aside for rework shall be reinspected and found acceptable before being passed on.

5.2.4   Final inspection

Final inspection is carried out by the fee-earner, on completion of a matter, to ensure that he or she has carried out the work which was agreed initially. Fee-earners' performance in this regard shall be annually appraised by Mr R.T. Hitchcock.

HITCHCOCK, SIMPSON, HARGRAVE, COKE & LITTLETON
QUALITY ASSURANCE PROCEDURE 10 (QAP 10)

LEGAL REFERENCE SYSTEM

AMENDMENT RECORD

This procedure is a mandatory requirement and forms part of the approved documented quality system.

Alterations are not permitted without the prior approval of Mr R.T. Hitchcock.

Issue	Date	Approved	Summary of change

HITCHCOCK, SIMPSON, HARGRAVE, COKE & LITTLETON
QUALITY ASSURANCE PROCEDURE 10 (QAP 10)

LEGAL REFERENCE SYSTEM

1 PURPOSE

The purpose of this procedure is to define the requirements for a legal reference system.

2 ASSOCIATED DOCUMENTS

Hitchcock, Simpson, Hargrave, Coke & Littleton Quality Assurance Manual, section 14.

3 RESPONSIBILITY

Mr R.T. Hitchcock is responsible for the authorisation, and distribution control, of the Quality Assurance Manual and supporting quality assurance procedures.

Mr S.P. Littleton is responsible for the preparation, retention and distribution of the Quality Assurance Manual and supporting quality assurance procedures to Mr Hitchcock's requirements.

Mr R.T. Hitchcock, or anyone he may designate, shall be responsible for maintaining up-to-date legal reference material necessary for the work undertaken by Hitchcock, Simpson, Hargrave, Coke & Littleton.

All staff shall be responsible for the proper care of legal reference material. Fee earners shall be responsible for reporting any legal reference material which is found to be out of date or incomplete and for providing copies of written research for use in the legal reference system as described below.

4 SCOPE

This procedure applies to all legal reference material used in the practice of law. It applies equally to such legal reference material whether owned by Hitchcock, Simpson, Hargrave, Coke & Littleton or on loan.

5 METHOD

5.1 Requirement

Hitchcock, Simpson, Hargrave, Coke & Littleton shall maintain a legal reference system, or have easy access to a legal reference system, sufficient to allow fee-earners to engage competently in the practice of law undertaken by Hitchcock, Simpson, Hargrave, Coke & Littleton.

All in-house legal reference material shall be kept up to date and shall be stored in the library. Any borrowed legal reference material shall be checked to make sure it is up to date.

All in-house legal reference material shall be catalogued in such a manner as to provide practitioners with ease of access to material in the collection.

Copies of all research documents generated within the practice shall be maintained and catalogued in the library.

5.2 Audit

The needs of the practice, with regard to legal reference material, shall be regularly audited and additions to the collection shall be made when required.

5.3 In-house generated research documents

When a fee-earner completes a research document (e.g., memorandum, brief), he or she shall direct that a copy is made for placement in the library as part of the legal reference system. The fee-earner shall complete a catalogue card to accompany the document. This card (an example is attached in annex 1) shall contain classification information including: broad area of law (e.g., property law), specific area of law (e.g., landlord and tenant), subject of research (e.g., tenant's duty to repair and maintain premises), date document written and author. The research document copy and the form shall be sent to the library where an individual, assigned responsibility for the library, shall place the document in a labelled binder, assign a catalogue number to the document (indicated on the document and on the catalogue card) and file the catalogue card in a catalogue.

5.4 Records

A record of all legal reference material in the library shall be kept in a catalogue. These records shall show the following details for each item in the collection: classification of material; catalogue number; title of publication, author of publication, publisher and date of publication.

5.5 Identification

After cataloguing, a 'catalogue number' label shall be placed on the item. Any reference material not bearing a 'catalogue number' label shall be regarded as being not catalogued.

5.6 Storage and handling

All legal reference material shall be handled and used with care. Defects shall be immediately reported by the user.

5.7 Mechanical equipment

All mechanical equipment used to access legal reference material (e.g., computers, microfilm readers) shall be inspected regularly to confirm operational effectiveness. A record of inspections shall be kept indicating date of inspection, person conducting inspection, problems found and remedial action taken.

5.8 Qualifications for use of equipment

All personnel using equipment to access legal research material shall have the appropriate experience, or training, to carry out the work to the required standards. If a new standard of skill is required for a particular item of equipment, Mr R.T. Hitchcock will review the requirements and arrange appropriate training.

5.9 Borrowed legal research material

Where legal research material is borrowed, then a check must be made before use to substantiate that it is up to date.

HITCHCOCK, SIMPSON, HARGRAVE, COKE & LITTLETON
ANNEX 1 TO QAP 10
LEGAL REFERENCE SYSTEM

PROPERTY LAW	Landlord and Tenant
tenant's duty to repair and maintain premises	
23 March 1995	Miss B.F. Sears

HITCHCOCK, SIMPSON, HARGRAVE, COKE & LITTLETON
QUALITY ASSURANCE PROCEDURE 11 (QAP 11)

PROBLEM REPORTING

AMENDMENT RECORD

This procedure is a mandatory requirement and forms part of the approved documented quality system.

Alterations are not permitted without the prior approval of Mr R.T. Hitchcock.

Issue	Date	Approved	Summary of change

HITCHCOCK, SIMPSON, HARGRAVE, COKE & LITTLETON
QUALITY ASSURANCE PROCEDURE 11 (QAP 11)

PROBLEM REPORTING

1 PURPOSE

The purpose of this procedure is to ensure that work that does not conform to specified requirements is prevented from inadvertent use.

2 ASSOCIATED DOCUMENTS

Hitchcock, Simpson, Hargrave, Coke & Littleton Quality Assurance Manual, section 16.
Quality Assurance Procedure 9, Inspection.

3 RESPONSIBILITY

All fee-earners and support staff are responsible for controlling non-conforming work product under their control.
All staff are responsible for reporting any work found to be deficient of requirements.
Mr S.P. Littleton is responsible for the issue and control of this procedure.

4 SCOPE

This procedure applies to all work carried out by Hitchcock, Simpson, Hargrave, Coke & Littleton.

5 METHOD

5.1 Identification

It is essential that all non-conforming work is clearly identified with a description of the defect/s and, as appropriate, the file number (e.g., an old draft of a contract is stamped 'superseded').
When the inadequacy is identified, the work product shall be clearly marked describing the defects (e.g., 'superseded', 'specimen only').
The procedure for identifying non-conforming items at goods inwards is described in QAP 7.

5.2 Action on non-conforming work

Where non-conforming work product is unintentional, it shall be brought to the attention of the person or persons who produced the work to determine the reason(s) for non-conformance.

5.3 Records

Mr R.T. Hitchcock shall arrange for records of unintentional non-conforming work-product to be maintained. These shall be retained for one year.

HITCHCOCK, SIMPSON, HARGRAVE, COKE & LITTLETON
QUALITY ASSURANCE PROCEDURE 12 (QAP 12)

CORRECTIVE ACTION

AMENDMENT RECORD

This procedure is a mandatory requirement and forms part of the approved documented quality system.

Alterations are not permitted without the prior approval of Mr R.T. Hitchcock.

Issue	Date	Approved	Summary of change

HITCHCOCK, SIMPSON, HARGRAVE, COKE & LITTLETON
QUALITY ASSURANCE PROCEDURE 12 (QAP 12)

CORRECTIVE ACTION

1 PURPOSE

The purpose of this procedure is to ensure that non-conformance to client requirements is reduced to a minimum.

2 ASSOCIATED DOCUMENTS

Hitchcock, Simpson, Hargrave, Coke & Littleton Quality Assurance Manual, section 17.
Quality Assurance Procedure 1, Quality System Audit and Review.

3 RESPONSIBILITY

Mr R.T. Hitchcock is responsible for: the investigation of customer complaints, investigation of causes of defective work and initiation of appropriate corrective action.
All employees are responsible for the reduction of non-conformance wherever possible.
Mr S.P. Littleton is responsible for the issue and control of this procedure.

4 SCOPE

This procedure applies to all work carried out by Hitchcock, Simpson, Hargrave, Coke & Littleton.

5 METHOD

5.1 Prevention

All Hitchcock, Simpson, Hargrave, Coke & Littleton client instructions shall be checked before work commences, to ensure that the instructions are clear, that the client's requirements are understood, and that the quality plan is appropriate. In the event of ambiguity or other problems, the necessary documents shall be discussed with the originator or client before work commences.
It is important to ensure that appropriately trained and/or qualified people are allocated to the work, and that legal reference materials are available suitable for undertaking the work. Potential problems should be reviewed, preventive action taken, and contingent action taken, appropriate to the degree of risk encountered.

5.2   Occurrence

In the event of non-conformance arising, immediate action is to be taken to investigate the cause and define the corrective action to be taken. The corrective action shall be followed through to completion, to ensure its effectiveness and to prevent recurrence. Any changes in procedures resulting from corrective action shall be implemented and recorded.

5.3   Customer Complaints

Any work that is the subject of complaint by the client shall be fully investigated by Mr R.T. Hitchcock, who shall determine the reasons for complaint and take corrective action on the items concerned and, as necessary, on the process and inspection procedures. He shall prepare a report for the quality review team (see QAP 1) clearly describing the problem, the causes and the corrective actions taken to ensure future compliance with all quality requirements (see annex 1).

5.4   Causes and corrective action

The amount of noncomplying work may be reduced by:

   (a)   clearer instructions or quality plans,
   (b)   improved client and outside firm or counsel liaison,
   (c)   improved goods inward inspection,
   (d)   improved outside firm, counsel, expert or services provider selection,
   (e)   identifying and checking that legal reference materials are suitable for the work undertaken.

Defective workmanship can be reduced by:

   (a)   improved training,
   (b)   better working instructions,
   (c)   workforce — better understanding of individual responsibility for quality,
   (d)   possibly better research materials,
   (e)   improved supervision and management.

5.5   Review and records

Reports of non-conformance and actions taken for correction and to ensure non-recurrence, shall be tabled at quality assurance review meetings (*see* QAP 1). Records as detailed above shall be retained for one year or as may be required by contract.

HITCHCOCK, SIMPSON, HARGRAVE, COKE & LITTLETON
ANNEX 1 TO QAP 12

WORK PROBLEM REPORT

Originator .... Date ....

Description of problem:

Probable cause/s:

Preventive and corrective action/s taken

Signed .... Date ....

HITCHCOCK, SIMPSON, HARGRAVE, COKE & LITTLETON
QUALITY ASSURANCE PROCEDURE 13 (QAP 13)

SAFEGUARDING OF DOCUMENTS AND MATERIAL

AMENDMENT RECORD

This procedure is a mandatory requirement and forms part of the approved documented quality system.

Alterations are not permitted without the prior approval of Mr R.T. Hitchcock.

Issue	Date	Approved	Summary of change

HITCHCOCK, SIMPSON, HARGRAVE, COKE & LITTLETON
QUALITY ASSURANCE PROCEDURE 13 (QAP 13)

SAFEGUARDING OF DOCUMENTS AND MATERIAL

1 PURPOSE

The purpose of this procedure is to define the requirements for the handling, storage and protection of documents and material.

2 ASSOCIATED DOCUMENTS

Hitchcock, Simpson, Hargrave, Coke & Littleton Quality Assurance Manual, section 18.

3 RESPONSIBILITY

All fee-earners are responsible for the operation of this procedure with regard to cases assigned to them.

All employees are responsible for care in handling documents and material under their control.

Mr S.P. Littleton is responsible for the issue and control of this procedure.

4 SCOPE

This procedure applies to all on-site documents and material under Hitchcock, Simpson, Hargrave, Coke & Littleton's control.

5 METHOD

5.1 Handling

Documents and material shall only be handled by appropriately qualified authorised personnel. Care shall be exercised to ensure that they are correctly handled (in a way that avoids damage), stored and maintained.

Care shall be taken to ensure that documents and material being used are handled carefully, identified as the work progresses, and protected and preserved as may be required by contract to prevent deterioration and facilitate further use.

5.2 Storage

All documents and material being used shall be stored in a manner appropriate to their value, type, condition, application and ability to withstand environmental conditions. The condition of documents and material in storage shall be assessed at appropriate intervals. All documents and material entered into and retrieved from storage will be recorded in the appropriate storage register.

5.3 Packaging

Appropriate packaging shall be used wherever necessary to maintain the condition of documents and material, and to prevent deterioration. Where required by the contract or quality plan, documents and material shall have appropriate packaging, marking and preservation to ensure adequate protection during delivery.

5.4 Delivery

Where it is a requirement of contract, transportation and delivery may be completed by Hitchcock, Simpson, Hargrave, Coke & Littleton, in which case the responsibility of proper handling and protection shall remain with the Firm until the customer accepts delivery.

HITCHCOCK, SIMPSON, HARGRAVE, COKE & LITTLETON
QUALITY ASSURANCE PROCEDURE 14 (QAP 14)

QUALITY RECORDS

AMENDMENT RECORD

This procedure is a mandatory requirement and forms part of the approved documented quality system.

Alterations are not permitted without the prior approval of Mr R.T. Hitchcock.

Issue	Date	Approved	Summary of change

HITCHCOCK, SIMPSON, HARGRAVE, COKE & LITTLETON
QUALITY ASSURANCE PROCEDURE 14 (QAP 14)

QUALITY RECORDS

1 PURPOSE

The purpose of this procedure is to ensure that records are maintained to demonstrate achievement of the required quality and the effective operation of the quality system.

2 ASSOCIATED DOCUMENTS

Hitchcock, Simpson, Hargrave, Coke & Littleton Quality Assurance Manual, section 19.

3 RESPONSIBILITY

All fee-earners are responsible for the records of work and material relating to cases to which they have been assigned as defined in the relevant procedures.
   Mr S.P. Littleton is responsible for the issue and control of this procedure.

4 SCOPE

This procedure applies to all quality records at Hitchcock, Simpson, Hargrave, Coke & Littleton.

5 METHOD

5.1 Definitions

The specific type of records to be kept and the contents in each area of quality assurance are defined in:

   (a)   the quality assurance manual,
   (b)   the quality assurance procedures.

5.2 Audit and review

Audit investigation and analysis of quality records forms part of the quality system review (see QAP 1).

5.3   Records

The purposes of records in the principal areas of quality assurance are:

(a)   instruction review — to ensure that all aspects of a contract are carefully considered before taking on a commitment and to record the circumstances then obtaining;

(b)   goods inward inspection — the records made at goods inward inspection enable a continuous evaluation of suppliers' quality and delivery date performance to be made, and to record the movements of client-supplied and other material;

(c)   stores records serve the principal purposes of stock control and identification of materials;

(d)   work process records are important for confirmation of client and legal requirements and for future reference in the case of any client complaint or product failure;

(e)   stage and final inspection — audit and analysis of these records enable management to detect deficiencies in work, work process problem areas, and training requirements;

(f)   legal reference material records show what reports, statutes, journals, treatises and reference books are needed to permit the Firm's fee-earners to engage competently in their practice of law.

5.4   Retention of records

All records shall be retained for a minimum period of one year or as required by the procedure or by the client contract. This does not waive the Firm's requirement to retain legal documents for a statutory period.

5.5   Audit, review and analysis of records

These are described in QAP 1, Quality System Audit and Review.

HITCHCOCK, SIMPSON, HARGRAVE, COKE & LITTLETON
QUALITY ASSURANCE PROCEDURE 15 (QAP 15)

TRAINING

AMENDMENT RECORD

This procedure is a mandatory requirement and forms part of the approved documented quality system.

Alterations are not permitted without the prior approval of Mr R.T. Hitchcock.

Issue	Date	Approved	Summary of change

HITCHCOCK, SIMPSON, HARGRAVE, COKE & LITTLETON
QUALITY ASSURANCE PROCEDURE 15 (QAP 15)

TRAINING

1 PURPOSE

The purpose of this procedure is to identify training needs for all activities affecting quality, to provide the training required, and to maintain appropriate records.

2 ASSOCIATED DOCUMENTS

Hitchcock, Simpson, Hargrave, Coke & Littleton Quality Assurance Manual, section 21.

3 RESPONSIBILITY

All fee-earners are responsible for:

(a) the identification of training needs of those reporting to them against the requirements for satisfactory performance of the work, and
(b) determining standards of satisfactory performance in their area of control.

Mr R.T. Hitchcock has overall responsibility for:

(a) identifying the way in which tasks and operations affect the Firm's quality in total,
(b) planning and arranging appropriate specific training,
(c) planning and arranging general quality awareness programmes, and
(d) recording the training carried out.

Mr S.P. Littleton is responsible for the issue and control of this procedure.

4 SCOPE

This procedure applies to all training requirements at Hitchcock, Simpson, Hargrave, Coke & Littleton.

5 METHOD

5.1 Policy

It is the policy of Hitchcock, Simpson, Hargrave, Coke & Littleton that all employees shall be trained and developed to enable them to do their existing job (or in the case of new employees, the job for which they were engaged) to the full extent of their ability and to the satisfaction of clients. It is also the policy of the Firm that all fee-earners meet the continuing professional development requirements of their appropriate professional body.

In addition, employees who demonstrate potential for more advanced work shall be encouraged and assisted to develop that potential so far as can be accommodated by the needs of the Firm.

5.2   Assessment

Each employee shall be assessed by Mr R.T. Hitchcock against the tasks and/or operations required for satisfactory performance of their work, and the results entered on to a 'state of training' analysis sheet (annex 1).

5.3   Using the analysis sheet

(a)   Enter the names of staff down the left-hand column.

(b)   Enter the different activities, or parts of activities, of the work of the Firm across the top.

(c)   Show who can do what to what standards by entering in the relevant boxes as shown in annex 1 so that it is easily seen who can do what, and to give better cover in the case of absence.

(d)   Enter continuing professional development credit hours earned each year.

5.4   Updating

The analysis sheets shall be added to for new people and new activities.

5.5   Training

Where training is required, it shall be brought to the attention of Mr R.T. Hitchcock, who shall arrange for the training to the required level to be carried out.

5.6   Records

As each part of the training is completed, Mr R.T. Hitchcock shall amend the training records accordingly.

HITCHCOCK, SIMPSON, HARGRAVE, COKE & LITTLETON
ANNEX 1 TO QAP 15
'STATE OF TRAINING' ANALYSIS SHEET

Name	Work Activity						CPD Hours

Key

Has not done this activity:

Under training:

Can do this activity but requires supervision:

Can do this activity without supervision:

Is capable of training others in this activity:

Seems untrainable in this activity:

HITCHCOCK, SIMPSON, HARGRAVE, COKE & LITTLETON
QUALITY ASSURANCE PROCEDURE 16 (QAP 16)

WORK FOLLOW-UP

AMENDMENT RECORD

This procedure is a mandatory requirement and forms part of the approved documented quality system.

Alterations are not permitted without the prior approval of Mr R.T. Hitchcock.

Issue	Date	Approved	Summary of change

HITCHCOCK, SIMPSON, HARGRAVE, COKE & LITTLETON
QUALITY ASSURANCE PROCEDURE 16 (QAP 16)

WORK FOLLOW-UP

1 PURPOSE

The purpose of this procedure is to ensure that agreed follow-up work is carried out and monitored within the quality system.

2 ASSOCIATED DOCUMENTS

Hitchcock, Simpson, Hargrave, Coke & Littleton Quality Assurance Manual, section 22.

3 RESPONSIBILITY

All fee-earners are responsible for:

    (a)   the identification and fulfilment of follow-up needs; and
    (b)   determining standards of satisfactory performance in their area of control for follow-up work.

    Mr R.T. Hitchcock has overall responsibility for making sure that follow-up needs are correctly identified and fulfilled.
    Mr S.P. Littleton is responsible for the issue and control of this procedure.

4 SCOPE

This procedure applies to all follow-up work requirements (e.g., advice previously rendered which has been rendered inaccurate or insufficient due to changes in law, the need to keep clients and client employees up to date on changes in the law which affects their work etc.) at Hitchcock, Simpson, Hargrave, Coke & Littleton.

5 METHOD

5.1 Policy

It is the policy of Hitchcock, Simpson, Hargrave, Coke & Littleton that all fee-earners shall identify and fulfil the work follow-up needs of clients.

5.2   Assessment

Each fee-earner shall indicate follow-up needs, with reference to cases worked on, in the quality assurance plan relevant to that case.

5.3   Planning

Each fee earner shall establish quality plans for general follow-up work not pertaining to individual cases. These quality plans shall include the names of people to receive follow-up information, the type of information to be rendered and the method for communicating said information.

5.4   Records

Fee-earners shall maintain records of what follow-up information is communicated to whom, and when it was communicated.

Chapter 6

The ISO 9001 Registration Process

A firm aiming for ISO 9001 registration should apply for assessment when it has had enough experience of the implemented quality assurance systems to feel confident with them, when it has carried out internal audits and reviews of the whole documented quality system and when it has records which demonstrate that the requirements of the standard are being met. The length of time taken to reach this stage will vary from firm to firm; it could be as short as six months where comparable systems previously existed, and could be as long as two years in some cases. It is sensible not to wait too long, since enthusiasm may wane.

When you think you are nearly ready, prepare three or four invitations to quote to send to appropriate certification bodies (Appendix II). The letters should set out some of the background to your quality assurance project — for example, how long the project has been going, the size and facilities of your practice — which will assist the certification body to prepare a quotation and allocate suitably experienced assessors. In addition, say when you will be ready for assessment and ask when the assessment can be carried out — some bodies have queuing time in certain areas of specialisation.

In the UK, any business seeking registration should ensure that the body it goes to is accredited by the National Accreditation Council for Certification Bodies (NACCB), an independent body operating under the auspices of the President of the Board of Trade. It represents, *inter alia*, government departments with major purchasing and legislative requirements, the Confederation of British Industry, the Trades Union Congress, professional institutions, insurance and inspection interests. The Council undertakes the impartial assessment of certification bodies applying for government accreditation. After accreditation, they are subject to regulation and continuous assessment by the NACCB. A complete list of accredited certification bodies, complete with addresses, telephone and fax numbers etc., is given in the DTI's *UK Register of Quality Assessed Companies*, to be found in the reference section of most public libraries.

Because the business of registering to ISO 9001 has expanded by leaps and bounds in recent years there are many more certification bodies than formerly; in February 1994 there were 33 accredited certification bodies in the UK, compared to six in 1987, and their commercial terms have become highly competitive. When considering which body to register with, there are some important points to note:

(a)   invite a competitive tender and take price, quality and delivery into account as with any other supplier;

(b)   consider whether the certification body is capable of assessing your practice;

(c)   check their 'scope of accreditation' in the listings, because some are highly specialised;

(d)   judge whether they are responsive to your own requirements;

(e)   determine if their literature is user-friendly and the paperwork simple;

(f)   note if they reply to your letters promptly, and if their quotation is simple and reasonably priced; and,

(g)   determine if they can do the assessment when you want it.

Bear in mind that they are all operating to exactly the same standard, ISO 9001, and all are of equal merit although some of the names are better known than others. Many operate simplified and less expensive schemes specifically for small businesses. It could be important to check that the one you eventually go for will be acceptable to, and/or compatible with, your major clients, should this be a consideration for your practice. When completing the application form, it should be made clear what you want the scope of the registration to be — if there are some offices or activities you do not want to include, for example, because they are not yet up to standard, they should be omitted at this stage and may be added later.

Most certification bodies have their own identifying symbols which can be used by registered organisations of assessed capability on stationery and for marketing purposes generally. The DTI's list referred to earlier also shows assessed organisations and their products and services, and on completion of satisfactory assessment and subsequent registration your practice can be added to the list — another marketing advantage.

The assessors employed by certification bodies have to have extensive business or industry experience together with appropriate educational qualifications and considerable understanding of ISO 9001 : 1994 and its application, as well as having successfully undertaken a Registration Board for Assessors approved lead assessor course and examination. Agreement on uniform requirements for training courses for assessor registration exists between the UK, the USA, Australia and New Zealand preparatory to reaching agreement on mutual recognition of certification bodies.

The way assessments are approached varies slightly from one certification body to another, but all follow the same basic pattern. First, the background of the business is considered and the amount of time and the number of people required for the assessment are estimated. These resources may range from one assessor for one day to, say, five people for a week or more for large enterprises. At the start of the assessment, an opening meeting with the management of the firm is held by the lead assessor. The scope and timing of the assessment will be discussed, so that it is clear between the parties what the subsequent registration will cover and how long the assessor/s will take to complete their work. A guide may be allocated by the organisation to assist the assessor/s.

The first task of the assessor is to ascertain whether the documented quality system is comprehensive and meets the requirements of the ISO 9001 standard. Some certification bodies ask for documentation to be sent to them and assess this before visiting the practice offices. The assessment then moves on to the second phase, which is to see whether what is actually done follows the documented procedures. In doing this, members of staff at all levels may be asked questions concerning the work; it is important for people to understand that it is not the individual that is being assessed, it is the documented quality system.

Should a major discrepancy or non-conformity (a failure to comply with a clause of the standard or a total breakdown of an element of the quality system) arise during the assessment, then the management is informed immediately. The assessment may then be continued for the organisation to be able to see the total results or ended at that point. Major non-conformances mean that registration cannot go ahead; they require corrective action and a complete reassessment.

As the assessment proceeds, a short meeting with management is held at the end of each day to report progress; a closing meeting is held at the end to discuss findings — a written report will either be presented at this point or will follow. If no major non-conformities are found, then the organisation will be recommended for registration, subject to any minor non-conformities found being addressed and corrected by the management within a fixed period of time. The number of continuing assessment visits each year, and the number of days required for each visit form part of the registration recommendation. Some certification bodies require a complete reassessment after a number of years, others use a rolling re-assessment approach.

The assessment is often viewed with apprehension by organisations, as being akin to sitting examinations. It is very straightforward, however: the assessors are experienced and are selected and trained to put people at their ease while still achieving the objectives of the assessment. They are there to assess the system, not the people and they are looking at only two things — does the documented quality system meet the standard, and do people do what they say they do? Remember, too, that the certification body has a financial incentive to help your practice achieve the registration requirements.

Most organisations pass assessment first time, usually after minor discrepancies have been put right. Where this does not happen, the causes are usually not difficult to find.

The most common reason for failure is lack of management commitment. This can show itself in a number of ways, and quickly becomes obvious to an experienced assessor. It can be revealed even at the assessment opening meeting, by management boredom, off-handedness, lack of understanding or even open disagreement between the managers of the firm. It can show itself in that the documented quality system shows what the writers think, or hope, happens, rather than what really does happen. When compared with the actuality, on assessment, it becomes obvious that the procedures have been put together without understanding of, or reference to, the standard — this often happens where a system has been bought in from elsewhere and put in without effort or proper adaptation. The assessor will look for *objective evidence* that what the documentation says *actually happens*.

The next most common reason is failure to carry out audit, review and corrective action. These requirements are absolutely fundamental to ISO 9001. A system is almost never absolutely right when first written, and it is by the application of audit that procedures can be corrected and refined with the experience of application; management review ensures that the entire quality system is suitable and effective for its purpose. The disciplines of drawing up an audit plan and allocating the resources needed, implementing it on the due dates, implementing the corrective actions required and ensuring that they are working as intended are ones which should quickly and easily become a way of life for a quality organisation and are arguably, together with review, the best possible demonstration of a high degree of management policy, control and commitment.

Other common reasons for failing to pass assessment are having inadequate documentation and failing to update the procedures. This can happen where the reasons for having procedures are not properly understood, or where the resources needed to produce and maintain them have not been allocated. The rule of thumb is to write procedures against each of the requirements of ISO 9001, ensure that they are used and that they are kept up to date. If there is more than one way of doing something, but only one way is right, then a procedure is required — if that way changes, then the procedure must be changed to incorporate that valuable learning and experience into the organisation. Where procedures are allowed to become out of step with actual practice, they will become discredited and will just not be used.

One last common reason is the failure to keep sufficient records; this problem is usually confined to organisations which do not ordinarily keep many records, or even in some cases, where there are illiteracy problems. Neither of these is liable to cause problems in law practices.

Probably the best way of introducing a quality system is to use an outside consultant. Qualified and experienced consultants can bring a breadth of experience to the task of helping a practice comply with ISO 9001. They can undertake and provide guidance on some of the most difficult quality assurance responsibilities including: explaining quality assurance management to the members of a practice, drafting a documented quality assurance system customised to a particular practice's needs, helping implement the system, advising on the choice of a certification body and arranging for assessment at the appropriate time. In addition, consultants can provide a catalyst for change and an incentive to keep the project moving, offer objective advice, and provide specialised training where required.

The use of a consultant can be cost-effective. Most quality assurance management consultants are less expensive than lawyers and can implement a practice's quality assurance objectives in significantly less time than a practice could do it itself. An experienced consultant will know what certification bodies look for and can save practices from wasting time on unnecessary tasks. As with any other supplier, a firm should consider whether the consultant offers value for money and will be effective in helping it meet the desired results.

It is extremely important to ensure that the consultant to be used fits well with the practice's style, and will be able to work with the practice management and inspire the enthusiam and support of all the employees for the quality assurance initiative. In this context, it is well to beware of some consultancies which send high-powered executives along to make the sale, then follow up with trainees to do the work.

In initial discussions, draft terms of reference should be drawn up by the consultant, setting out broadly what it is that the consultant is expected to achieve. This should be supported by a project plan giving target times agreed between the parties — these can vary widely because of the differences in size and scope of projects and the extent to which the practice will be doing at least some of the work. The Law Society publishes The *Directory of Consultants for Solicitors* and appendix A of that document gives an excellent code of practice to follow when considering the use of consultants.

Typical terms of reference for the introduction of an ISO 9001 documented quality system are as follows:

1. INTRODUCTION

Gives the background to the proposed project to ensure that the consultant has a correct understanding of the practice's operations and requirements.

2. PROJECT OBJECTIVES

To provide advice and practical assistance to the practice in the design, development and implementation of a quality management system to meet the requirements of ISO 9001 : 1994.

3. PROGRAMME OF WORK

Task 1: To carry out a review of the practice's current activities against the requirements of ISO 9001 : 1994 and prepare a report. To review this report with management and agree an initial project programme.

Task 2: To prepare a draft Quality Assurance Manual referencing, where appropriate, supporting procedures and other documentation to meet the requirements of the standard. To review the Quality Assurance Manual with management and advise and assist in implementation.

Task 3: To identify and assist in the preparation of all necessary supporting quality assurance procedures and advise on the preparation of any other supporting documentation.

Task 4: To review the quality assurance procedures with management and assist and advise on their implementation and integration with any other system operating in the practice.

Task 5: To give presentations to staff on quality assurance, the requirements of ISO 9001 : 1994, and their part in achieving registration.

Task 6: To conduct a final survey of the complete quality assurance system on completion of the project and produce a report identifying the progress in implementation, noting any areas of non-compliance, with recommendations for remedial action plus, if appropriate, a proposed action plan for work that is outstanding to meet the required level.

Task 7: To produce the final report and, if appropriate, hold a meeting with the practice to discuss the project.

Further information should include the name of the consultant who will be carrying out the work; a project programme showing the start and estimated finish dates for each stage; clauses covering termination, damages or loss; confidentiality etc., and payment arrangements.

Registration to ISO 9001 can be a highly motivating experience for a legal practice, demonstrating as it does that it has been found, by a completely independent and objective third party, to be operating in an efficient manner to an established and internationally recognised standard. However, that is the least part of the story; there are many other benefits to secure. Working in a quality way — evaluating existing practices and adopting the best of new ones — strengthens the direction of every member of the practice towards a better service to the client. This will ultimately and inevitably bring monetary benefits to the practice. Practices which have implemented quality assurance systems have, for example, achieved significant reductions in operating costs, increased the productivity of employees and decreased the cost of professional indemnity insurance. ISO 9001 registration can help a practice attract more business and better manage the business once obtained. Registration can also be particularly effective when used as a marketing tool abroad in that it demonstrates that a practice, even a small or provincial one, operates to internationally accepted standards and uses internationally accepted concepts. ISO 9001 is a valuable tool for any legal practice interested in surviving and succeeding in an increasingly competitive and international legal market.

Appendix I

International Standard.
Quality Systems — Model for Quality Assurance in Design, Development, Production, Installation and Servicing (ISO 9001 : 1994)*

4   QUALITY SYSTEM REQUIREMENTS

4.1   Management responsibility

4.1.1   *Quality policy*
The supplier's management with executive responsibility shall define and document its policy for quality, including objectives for quality and its commitment to quality. The quality policy shall be relevant to the supplier's organizational goals and the expectations and needs of its customers. The supplier shall ensure that this policy is understood, implemented and maintained at all levels of the organization.

4.1.2   *Organization*

4.1.2.1   Responsibility and authority   The responsibility, authority and the interrelation of personnel who manage, perform and verify work affecting quality shall be defined and documented, particularly for personnel who need the organizational freedom and authority to:

(a)   initiate action to prevent the occurrence of any nonconformities relating to the product, process and quality system;

---

* Chapter 4 of ISO 9001 : 1994 has been reproduced with the permission of the International Organisation for Standardisation, ISO. The complete standard can be obtained from any ISO member or from the ISO Central Secretariat, Case Postale 56, CH-1211 Geneva 20, Switzerland. Copyright remains with ISO.

(b)   identify and record any problems relating to the product, process and quality system;

(c)   initiate, recommend or provide solutions through designated channels;

(d)   verify the implementation of solutions;

(e)   control further processing, delivery or installation of nonconforming product until the deficiency or unsatisfactory condition has been corrected.

4.1.2.2   Resources   The supplier shall identify resource requirements and provide adequate resources, including the assignment of trained personnel (see 4.18), for management, performance of work and verification activities including internal quality audits.

4.1.2.3   Management representative   The supplier's management with executive responsibility shall appoint a member of the supplier's own management who, irrespective of other responsibilities, shall have defined authority for

(a)   ensuring that a quality system is established, implemented and maintained in accordance with this International Standard, and

(b)   reporting on the performance of the quality system to the supplier's management for review and as a basis for improvement of the quality system.

NOTE 5   The responsibility of a management representative may also include liaison with external parties on matters relating to the supplier's quality system.

4.1.3   Management review

The supplier's management with executive responsibility shall review the quality system at defined intervals sufficient to ensure its continuing suitability and effectiveness in satisfying the requirements of this International Standard and the supplier's stated quality policy and objectives (see 4.1.1). Records of such reviews shall be maintained (see 4.16).

4.2   Quality system

4.2.1   General

The supplier shall establish, document and maintain a quality system as a means of ensuring that product conforms to specified requirements. The supplier shall prepare a quality manual covering the requirements of this International Standard. The quality manual shall include or make reference to the quality system procedures and outline the structure of the documentation used in the quality system.

NOTE 6   Guidance on quality manuals is given in ISO 10013.

4.2.2   Quality system procedures
The supplier shall

(a)   prepare documented procedures consistent with the requirements of this International Standard and the supplier's stated quality policy, and

(b)   effectively implement the quality system and its documented procedures.

For the purposes of this International Standard, the range and detail of the procedures that form part of the quality system shall be dependent upon the complexity of the work, the methods used, and the skills and training needed by personnel involved in carrying out the activity.

NOTE 7   Documented procedures may make reference to work instructions that define how an activity is performed.

4.2.3   Quality planning
The supplier shall define and document how the requirements for quality will be met. Quality planning shall be consistent with all other requirements of a supplier's quality system and shall be documented in a format to suit the supplier's method of operation.

The supplier shall give consideration to the following activities, as appropriate, in meeting the specified requirements for products, projects or contracts:

(a)   the preparation of quality plans;

(b)   the identification and acquisition of any controls, processes, equipment (including inspection and test equipment), fixtures, resources and skills that may be needed to achieve the required quality;

(c)   ensuring the compatibility of the design, the production process, installation, servicing, inspection and test procedures and the applicable documentation;

(d)   the updating, as necessary, of quality control, inspection and testing techniques, including the development of new instrumentation;

(e)   the identification of any measurement requirement involving capability that exceeds the known state of the art, in sufficient time for the needed capability to be developed;

(f)   the identification of suitable verification at appropriate stages in the realization of product;

(g)   the clarification of standards of acceptability for all features and requirements, including those which contain a subjective element;

(h)   the identification and preparation of quality records (see 4.16).

NOTE 8   The quality plans referred to see 4.2.3(a) may be in the form of a reference to the appropriate documented procedures that form an integral part of the supplier's quality system.

4.3   Contract review

4.3.1   General
The supplier shall establish and maintain documented procedures for contract review and for the coordination of these activities.

4.3.2   Review
Before submission of a tender, or the acceptance of a contract or order (statement of requirement), the tender, contract or order shall be reviewed by the supplier to ensure that:

(a)   the requirements are adequately defined and documented; where no written statement of requirement is available for an order received by verbal means, the supplier shall ensure that the order requirements are agreed before their acceptance;
(b)   any differences between the contract or order requirements and those in the tender are resolved;
(c)   the supplier has the capability to meet the contract or order requirements.

4.3.3   Amendment to a contract
The supplier shall identify how an amendment to a contract is made and correctly transferred to the functions concerned within the supplier's organization.

4.3.4 Records
Records of contract reviews shall be maintained (see 4.16).

NOTE 9   Channels for communication and interfaces with the customer's organization in these contract matters should be established.

4.4   Design control

4.4.1   General
The supplier shall establish and maintain documented procedures to control and verify the design of the product in order to ensure that the specified requirements are met.

4.4.2   Design and development planning
The supplier shall prepare plans for each design and development activity. The plans shall describe or reference these activities, and define responsibility for their implementation. The design and development activities shall be assigned to qualified personnel equipped with adequate resources. The plans shall be updated as the design evolves.

4.4.3 *Organizational and technical interfaces*
Organizational and technical interfaces between different groups which input into the design process shall be defined and the necessary information documented, transmitted and regularly reviewed.

4.4.4 *Design input*
Design input requirements relating to the product, including applicable statutory and regulatory requirements, shall be identified, documented and their selection reviewed by the supplier for adequacy. Incomplete, ambiguous or conflicting requirements shall be resolved with those responsible for imposing these requirements.

Design input shall take into consideration the results of any contract review activities.

4.4.5 *Design output*
Design output shall be documented and expressed in terms that can be verified and validated against design input requirements.

Design output shall:

    (a)   meet the design input requirements;
    (b)   contain or make reference to acceptance criteria;
    (c)   identify those characteristics of the design that are crucial to the safe and proper functioning of the product (e.g. operating, storage, handling, maintenance and disposal requirements).

Design output documents shall be reviewed before release.

4.4.6 *Design review*
At appropriate stages of design, formal documented reviews of the design results shall be planned and conducted. Participants at each design review shall include representatives of all functions concerned with the design stage being reviewed, as well as other specialist personnel, as required. Records of such reviews shall be maintained (see 4.16).

4.4.7 *Design verification*
At appropriate stages of design, design verification shall be performed to ensure that the design stage output meets the design stage input requirements. The design verification measures shall be recorded (see 4.16).

NOTE 10   In addition to conducting design reviews (see 4.4.6), design verification may include activities such as

—   performing alternative calculations,
—   comparing the new design with a similar proven design, if available,

— undertaking tests and demonstrations, and
— reviewing the design stage documents before release.

4.4.8 *Design validation*
Design validation shall be performed to ensure that product conforms to defined user needs and/or requirements.

NOTES
11   Design validation follows successful design verification (see 4.4.7).
12   Validation is normally performed under defined operating conditions.
13   Validation is normally performed on the final product, but may be necessary in earlier stages prior to product completion.
14   Multiple validations may be performed if there are different intended uses.

4.4.9 *Design changes*
All design changes and modifications shall be identified, documented, reviewed and approved by authorized personnel before their implementation.

4.5   Document and data control

4.5.1   *General*
The supplier shall establish and maintain documented procedures to control all documents and data that relate to the requirements of this International Standard including, to the extent applicable, documents of external origin such as standards and customer drawings.

NOTE 15   Documents and data can be in the form of any type of media, such as hard copy or electronic media.

4.5.2   *Document and data approval and issue*
The documents and data shall be reviewed and approved for adequacy by authorized personnel prior to issue. A master list or equivalent document control procedure identifying the current revision status of documents shall be established and be readily available to preclude the use of invalid and/or obsolete documents.
    This control shall ensure that:

(a)   the pertinent issues of appropriate documents are available at all locations where operations essential to the effective functioning of the quality system are performed;

(b)   invalid and/or obsolete documents are promptly removed from all points of issue or use, or otherwise assured against unintended use;

(c)   any obsolete documents retained for legal and/or knowledge-preservation purposes are suitably identified.

4.5.3 Document and data changes

Changes to documents and data shall be reviewed and approved by the same functions/organizations that performed the original review and approval, unless specifically designated otherwise. The designated functions/organizations shall have access to pertinent background information upon which to base their review and approval.

Where practicable, the nature of the change shall be identified in the document or the appropriate attachments.

4.6 Purchasing

4.6.1 General

The supplier shall establish and maintain documented procedures to ensure that purchased product . . . conforms to specified requirements.

4.6.2 Evaluation of subcontractors

The supplier shall:

(a) evaluate and select subcontractors on the basis of their ability to meet subcontract requirements including the quality system and any specific quality assurance requirements;

(b) define the type and extent of control exercised by the supplier over subcontractors. This shall be dependent upon the type of product, the impact of subcontracted product on the quality of final product and, where applicable, on the quality audit reports and/or quality records of the previously demonstrated capability and performance of subcontractors;

(c) establish and maintain quality records of acceptable subcontractors (see 4.16).

4.6.3 Purchasing data

Purchasing documents shall contain data clearly describing the product ordered, including where applicable:

(a) the type, class, grade or other precise identification;

(b) the title or other positive identification, and applicable issues of specifications, drawings, process requirements, inspection instructions and other relevant technical data, including requirements for approval or qualification of product, procedures, process equipment and personnel;

(c) the title, number and issue of the quality system standard to be applied.

The supplier shall review and approve purchasing documents for adequacy of the specified requirements prior to release.

4.6.4 *Verification of purchased product*

4.6.4.1 *Supplier verification at subcontractor's promises* Where the supplier proposes to verify purchased product at the subcontractor's premises, the supplier shall specify verification arrangements and the method of product release in the purchasing documents.

4.6.4.2 *Customer verification of subcontracted product* Where specified in the contract, the supplier's customer or the customer's representative shall be afforded the right to verify at the subcontractor's premises and the supplier's premises that subcontracted product conforms to specified requirements. Such verification shall not be used by the supplier as evidence of effective control of quality by the subcontractor.

Verification by the customer shall not absolve the supplier of the responsibility to provide acceptable product, nor shall it preclude subsequent rejection by the customer.

4.7 Control of customer-supplied product

The supplier shall establish and maintain documented procedures for the control of verification, storage and maintenance of customer-supplied product provided for incorporation into the supplies or for related activities. Any such product that is lost, damaged or is otherwise unsuitable for use shall be recorded and reported to the customer (see 4.16).

Verification by the supplier does not absolve the customer of the responsibility to provide acceptable product.

4.8 Product identification and traceability

Where appropriate, the supplier shall establish and maintain documented procedures for identifying the product by suitable means from receipt and during all stages of production, delivery and installation.

Where and to the extent that traceability is a specified requirement, the supplier shall establish and maintain documented procedures for unique identification of individual product or batches. This identification shall be recorded (see 4.16).

4.9 Process control

The supplier shall identify and plan the production, installation and servicing processes which directly affect quality and shall ensure that these processes are carried out under controlled conditions. Controlled conditions shall include the following:

(a) documented procedures defining the manner of production, installation and servicing, where the absence of such procedures could adversely affect quality;

(b) use of suitable production, installation and servicing equipment, and a suitable working environment;

(c) compliance with reference standards/codes, quality plans and/or documented procedures;

(d) monitoring and control of suitable process parameters and product characteristics;

(e) the approval of processes and equipment, as appropriate;

(f) criteria for workmanship, which shall be stipulated in the clearest practical manner (e.g. written standards, representative samples or illustrations);

(g) suitable maintenance of equipment to ensure continuing process capability.

Where the results of processes cannot be fully verified by subsequent inspection and testing of the product and where, for example, processing deficiencies may become apparent only after the product is in use, the processes shall be carried out by qualified operators and/or shall require continuous monitoring and control of process parameters to ensure that the specified requirements are met.

The requirements for any qualification of process operations, including associated equipment and personnel (see 4.18), shall be specified.

NOTE 16 Such processes requiring pre-qualification of their process capability are frequently referred to as special processes.

Records shall be maintained for qualified processes, equipment and personnel, as appropriate (see 4.16).

4.10 Inspection and testing

4.10.1 General
The supplier shall establish and maintain documented procedures for inspection and testing activities in order to verify that the specified requirements for the product are met. The required inspection and testing, and the records to be established, shall be detailed in the quality plan or documented procedures.

4.10.2 Receiving inspection and testing

4.10.2.1 The supplier shall ensure that incoming product is not used or processed (except in the circumstances described in 4.10.2.3) until it has been inspected or otherwise verified as conforming to specified requirements. Verification of conformance to the specified requirements shall be in accordance with the quality plan and/or documented procedures.

4.10.2.2   In determining the amount and nature of receiving inspection, consideration shall be given to the amount of control exercised at the subcontractor's premises and the recorded evidence of conformance provided.

4.10.2.3   Where incoming product is released for urgent production purposes prior to verification, it shall be positively identified and recorded (see 4.16) in order to permit immediate recall and replacement in the event of nonconformity to specified requirements.

4.10.3   In-process inspection and testing
The supplier shall:

(a)   inspect and test the product as required by the quality plan and/or documented procedures;

(b)   hold product until the required inspection and tests have been completed or necessary reports have been received and verified, except when product is released under positive-recall procedures (see 4.10.2.3). Release under positive-recall procedures shall not preclude the activities outlined in 4.10.3 (a).

4.10.4   Final inspection and testing
The supplier shall carry out all final inspection and testing in accordance with the quality plan and/or documented procedures to complete the evidence of conformance of the finished product to the specified requirements.

The quality plan and/or documented procedures for final inspection and testing shall require that all specified inspection and tests, including those specified either on receipt of product or in-process, have been carried out and that the results meet specified requirements.

No product shall be dispatched until all the activities specified in the quality plan and/or documented procedures have been satisfactorily completed and the associated data and documentation are available and authorized.

4.10.5   Inspection and test records
The supplier shall establish and maintain records which provide evidence that the product has been inspected and/or tested. These records shall show clearly whether the product has passed or failed the inspections and/or tests according to defined acceptance criteria. Where the product fails to pass any inspection and/or test, the procedures for control of nonconforming product shall apply (see 4.13).

Records shall identify the inspection authority responsible for the release of product (see 4.16).

4.11   Control of inspection, measuring and test equipment

4.11.1   General
The supplier shall establish and maintain documented procedures to control, calibrate and maintain inspection, measuring and test equipment (including test

software) used by the supplier to demonstrate the conformance of product to the specified requirements. Inspection, measuring and test equipment shall be used in a manner which ensures that the measurement uncertainty is known and is consistent with the required measurement capability.

Where test software or comparative references such as test hardware are used as suitable forms of inspection, they shall be checked to prove that they are capable of verifying the acceptability of product, prior to release for use during production, installation or servicing, and shall be rechecked at prescribed intervals. The supplier shall establish the extent and frequency of such checks and shall maintain records as evidence of control (see 4.16).

Where the availability of technical data pertaining to the inspection, measuring and test equipment is a specified requirement, such data shall be made available, when required by the customer or customer's representative, for verification that the inspection, measuring and test equipment is functionally adequate.

NOTE 17   For the purposes of this International Standard, the term 'measuring equipment' includes measurement devices.

4.11.2   Control procedure
The supplier shall:

(a)   determine the measurements to be made and the accuracy required, and select the appropriate inspection, measuring and test equipment that is capable of the necessary accuracy and precision;

(b)   identify all inspection, measuring and test equipment that can affect product quality, and calibrate and adjust them at prescribed intervals, or prior to use, against certified equipment having a known valid relationship to internationally or nationally recognized standards. Where no such standards exist, the basis used for calibration shall be documented;

(c)   define the process employed for the calibration of inspection, measuring and test equipment, including details of equipment type, unique identification, location, frequency of checks, check method, acceptance criteria and the action to be taken when results are unsatisfactory;

(d)   identify inspection, measuring and test equipment with a suitable indicator or approved identification record to show the calibration status;

(e)   maintain calibration records for inspection, measuring and test equipment (see 4.16);

(f)   assess and document the validity of previous inspection and test results when inspection, measuring or test equipment is found to be out of calibration;

(g)   ensure that the environmental conditions are suitable for the calibrations, inspections, measurements and tests being carried out;

(h)   ensure that the handling, preservation and storage of inspection, measuring and test equipment is such that the accuracy and fitness for use are maintained;

(i)   safeguard inspection, measuring and test facilities, including both test hardware and test software, from adjustments which would invalidate the calibration setting.

NOTE 18   The metrological confirmation system for measuring equipment given in ISO 10012 may be used for guidance.

4.12   Inspection and test status

The inspection and test status of product shall be identified by suitable means, which indicate the conformance or nonconformance of product with regard to inspection and tests performed. The identification of inspection and test status shall be maintained, as defined in the quality plan and/or documented procedures, throughout production, installation and servicing of the product to ensure that only product that has passed the required inspections and tests (or released under an authorized concession (see 4.13.2)) is dispatched, used or installed.

4.13   Control of nonconforming product

4.13.1   General
The supplier shall establish and maintain documented procedures to ensure that product that does not conform to specified requirements is prevented from unintended use or installation. This control shall provide for identification, documentation, evaluation, segregation (when practical), disposition of nonconforming product, and for notification to the functions concerned.

4.13.2   Review and disposition of nonconforming product
The responsibility for review and authority for the disposition of nonconforming product shall be defined.

Nonconforming product shall be reviewed in accordance with documented procedures. It may be

(a)   reworked to meet the specified requirements,
(b)   accepted with or without repair by concession,
(c)   regraded for alternative applications, or
(d)   rejected or scrapped.

Where required by the contract, the proposed use or repair of product (see 4.13.2(b)) which does not conform to specified requirements shall be reported for concession to the customer or customer's representative. The description of the nonconformity that has been accepted, and of repairs, shall be recorded to denote the actual condition (see 4.16).

Repaired and/or reworked product shall be reinspected in accordance with the quality plan and/or documented procedures.

4.14   Corrective and preventive action

4.14.1   General
The supplier shall establish and maintain documented procedures for implementing corrective and preventive action.

Any corrective or preventive action taken to eliminate the causes of actual or potential nonconformities shall be to a degree appropriate to the magnitude of problems and commensurate with the risks encountered.

The supplier shall implement and record any changes to the documented procedures resulting from corrective and preventive action.

4.14.2   Corrective action
The procedures for corrective action shall include:

(a)   the effective handling of customer complaints and reports of product nonconformities;

(b)   investigation of the cause of nonconformities relating to product, process and quality system, and recording the results of the investigation (see 4.16);

(c)   determination of the corrective action needed to eliminate the cause of nonconformities;

(d)   application of controls to ensure that corrective action is taken and that it is effective.

4.14.3   Preventive action
The procedures for preventive action shall include:

(a)   the use of appropriate sources of information such as processes and work operations which affect product quality, concessions, audit results, quality records, service reports and customer complaints to detect, analyse and eliminate potential causes of nonconformities;

(b)   determination of the steps needed to deal with any problems requiring preventive action;

(c)   initiation of preventive action and application of controls to ensure that it is effective;

(d)   ensuring that relevant information on actions taken is submitted for management review (see 4.1.3).

4.15   Handling, storage, packaging, preservation and delivery

4.15.1   General
The supplier shall establish and maintain documented procedures for handling, storage, packaging, preservation and delivery of product.

4.15.2 Handling
The supplier shall provide methods of handling product that prevent damage or deterioration.

4.15.3 Storage
The supplier shall use designated storage areas or stock rooms to prevent damage or deterioration of product, pending use or delivery. Appropriate methods for authorizing receipt to and dispatch from such areas shall be stipulated.

In order to detect deterioration, the condition of product in stock shall be assessed at appropriate intervals.

4.15.4 Packaging
The supplier shall control packing, packaging and marking processes (including materials used) to the extent necessary to ensure conformance to specified requirements.

4.15.5 Preservation
The supplier shall apply appropriate methods for preservation and segregation of product when the product is under the supplier's control.

4.15.6 Delivery
The supplier shall arrange for the protection of the quality of product after final inspection and test, Where contractually specified, this protection shall be extended to include delivery to destination.

4.16 Control of quality records

The supplier shall establish and maintain documented procedures for identification, collection, indexing, access, filing, storage, maintenance and disposition of quality records.

Quality records shall be maintained to demonstrate conformance to specified requirements and the effective operation of the quality system. Pertinent quality records from the subcontractor shall be an element of these data.

All quality records shall be legible and shall be stored and retained in such a way that they are readily retrievable in facilities that provide a suitable environment to prevent damage or deterioration and to prevent loss. Retention times of quality records shall be established and recorded. Where agreed contractually, quality records shall be made available for evaluation by the customer or the customer's representative for an agreed period.

NOTE 19   Records may be in the form of any type of media, such as hard copy or electronic media.

4.17 Internal quality audits

The supplier shall establish and maintain documented procedures for planning and implementing internal quality audits to verify whether quality activities and related results comply with planned arrangements and to determine the effectiveness of the quality system.

Internal quality audits shall be scheduled on the basis of the status and importance of the activity to be audited and shall be carried out by personnel independent of those having direct responsibility for the activity being audited.

The results of the audits shall be recorded (see 4.16) and brought to the attention of the personnel having responsibility in the area audited. The management personnel responsible for the area shall take timely corrective action on deficiencies found during the audit.

Follow-up audit activities shall verify and record the implementation and effectiveness of the corrective action taken (see 4.16).

NOTES

20   The results of internal quality audits form an integral part of the input to management review activities (see 4.1.3).

21   Guidance on quality system audits is given in ISO 10011.

4.18 Training

The supplier shall establish and maintain documented procedures for identifying training needs and provide for the training of all personnel performing activities affecting quality. Personnel performing specific assigned tasks shall be qualified on the basis of appropriate education, training and/or experience, as required. Appropriate records of training shall be maintained (see 4.16).

4.19 Servicing

Where servicing is a specified requirement, the supplier shall establish and maintain documented procedures for performing, verifying and reporting that the servicing meets the specified requirements.

4.20 Statistical techniques

4.20.1 Identification of need

The supplier shall identify the need for statistical techniques required for establishing, controlling and verifying process capability and product characteristics.

4.20.2   Procedures
The supplier shall establish and maintain documented procedures to implement and control the application of the statistical techniques identified in 4.20.1.

Appendix II

UK Accredited Certification Bodies Experienced in Legal Services Registration

Bureau Veritas Quality International Ltd
70 Borough High Street
London SE1 1XF
Tel: 0171 378 8113, Fax: 0171 378 8014

BSI Quality Assurance
PO Box 375
Milton Keynes MK14 6LL
Tel: 01908 220908, Fax: 01908 220671

Det Norske Veritas Quality Assurance Ltd
Palace House
3 Cathedral Street
London SE1 9DE
Tel: 0171 357 6080, Fax: 0171 357 6048

SOQAR Ltd
Metropolitan House
City Park Business Village
Cornbrook
Manchester M16 9HQ
Tel: 0161 877 6914, Fax: 0161 877 6915

Lloyd's Register Quality Assurance Ltd
Norfolk House
Wellesley Road
Croydon CR9 2DT
Tel: 0181 688 6883, Fax: 0181 681 8146

SGS Yarsley International Certification Services
Trowers Way
Redhill, Surrey RH1 2JN
Tel: 01737 768445/765070, Fax: 01737 772845

Bibliography

PRIMARY SOURCE MATERIAL

Best Practice: A Management Kit for Solicitors in Private Practice (London: The Law Society, 1993).

British Standard. Quality Vocabulary (ISO 8402) (Milton Keynes: British Standards Institution, 1987–91.

British Standard. Guide to the Economics of Quality (BS 6143) (Milton Keynes: British Standards Institution, 1990–2.

British Standard. Total Quality Management (BS 7850) (Milton Keynes: British Standards Institution, 1992–4.

British Standard. Quality Management and Quality Assurance Standards. Part 1. Guidelines for Selection and Use (BS EN ISO 9000–1 : 1994) (Milton Keynes: British Standards Institution, 1994). Formerly BS 5750 : Section 0.1.)

British Standard. Quality Management and Quality System Elements. Part 1. Guidelines (BS EN ISO 9004–1 : 1994) (Milton Keynes: British Standards Institution, 1994). Formerly BS 5750 : Section 0.2.)

British Standard. Quality Standard. Quality Systems. Model for Quality Assurance in Design, Development, Production, Installation and Servicing (BS EN ISO 9001 : 1994) (Milton Keynes: British Standards Institution, 1994). (Formerly BS 5750 : Part 1.)

British Standard. Guide to the use of BS EN ISO 9001 (BS 5750 : Part 4 : 1995) (Milton Keynes: British Standards Institution, 1995).

British Standard. Guide to Quality Management . . . for Services (BS 5750 : Part 8 : 1991) (Milton Keynes: British Standards Institution, 1991).

Consultation Paper Practice Management Standards (London: The Law Society, 1993).

Franchising: the Next Steps (London: Legal Aid Board, 1992).

Franchising Specification Draft for Consultation (London: Legal Aid Board, 1993).

International Standard. Quality systems - Model for Quality Assurance in Design, Development, Production, Installation and Servicing (ISO 9001 : 1994) (Geneva: ISO, 1994).

The Law Society's Solicitors' Office Manual (London: The Law Society, 1993).

Sherr, Avrom, Moorhead, Richard, and Paterson, Alan, *Transaction Criteria* (London: HMSO, 1992).

SECONDARY SOURCE MATERIAL

Collard, Ron, *Total Quality — Success through People* (London: Institute of Personnel Management, 1989).

Crosby, Philip B, *Quality without Tears* (New York: McGraw-Hill, 1984).

Deming, W. Edwards, *Quality, Productivity, and Competitive Position* (Cambridge, MA: Massachusetts Institute of Technology CAES, 1982).

Ishikawa, Kaoru, *Guide to Quality Control* (Tokyo: Asian Productivity Association, 1976).

Juran, Joseph M, *Managerial Breakthrough* (New York: McGraw-Hill, 1964).

Juran, Joseph M. (ed.) *Quality Control Handbook* 4th ed. (New York: McGraw-Hill, 1992).

Oakland, John S, *Total Quality Management* (Oxford: Heinemann, 1989).

Peters, Thomas J., and Waterman, Robert H., Jnr, *In Search of Excellence* (New York: Harper & Row, 1982).

Quality: a Briefing for Solicitors and BS 5750 Code of Quality Management for Solicitors (London: The Law Society, 1993). See pp. 54–62 for additional publications.

The Route Ahead: Comprehensive List of Publications and Videos (London: DTI, 1990).

Ernst & Young Quality Improvement Consultancy Group USA, *Total Quality: a Manager's Guide for the 90s* (New York: Kogan Page, 1990).

Index